30
KNITTED HEADBANDS
AND
EAR WARMERS

stylish designs for every occasion

JENISE HOPE

STACKPOLE
BOOKS

Guilford, Connecticut

Published by Stackpole Books
An imprint of Globe Pequot
Trade Division of The Rowman & Littlefield Publishing Group, Inc.
4501 Forbes Boulevard, Suite 200, Lanham, Maryland 20706

Distributed by NATIONAL BOOK NETWORK
800-462-6420

British Library Cataloguing in Publication Information available
Library of Congress Cataloging-in-Publication Data available

ISBN 978-0-8117-1741-0 (paperback)
ISBN 978-0-8117-6581-7 (e-book)

♾™ The paper used in this publication meets the minimum requirements of American National
Standard for Information Sciences—Permanence of Paper for Printed Library Materials, ANSI/NISO
Z39.48-1992.

First edition

Printed in the United States of America

Contents

Acknowledgments

The support and encouragement my parents offered when I first told them I was thinking of writing knitting patterns was key to my ever even giving it a try. None of us seriously thought it would grow the way it has, and they have rejoiced with me over every new success. My younger sisters all helped in many ways as I started out: They have sample-knit for me, made me dinners, and endured photoshoots on family vacations. While my family helped much less on this latest project, mostly due to my moving five hours away, I would not have written this book now if it were not for the encouragement they gave me at the beginning.

In this book, you'll see many beautiful photos, thanks to my friends who thought it a fun adventure to get up at five in the morning and head to the beach just after sunrise for photoshoots. None of us is a professional model—had you been there at our photoshoots, you would have thought us a group of friends just hanging out for the day, which we were. Days like those make me realize I have one of the best jobs in the world.

I have many old and new friends on Ravelry (ravelry.com). We hang out in my group, and occasionally some of them give me a hand by doing some knitting. I didn't knit all these headbands by myself. To Deb Taylor, RSJTA, Jerrill Spence, julieandco, Lori Veteto (hooknneedler), and Katherine Nguyen—thank you!

To everyone at Stackpole who has been working with me on the project— thank you!

And finally, to my husband: When I was negotiating the terms of the contract for this book, we were not even engaged yet. We bought yarn for the book on our honeymoon. The first photoshoot I did was pre-pregnancy, and the last was at seven months pregnant. As I type today, our baby is six months old, and she will be over a year by the time this book is published. Meanwhile, we've had "the book" going on in the background of our whole married life, and I am thankful you welcome it!

Introduction

As a knitter living in British Columbia, Canada, where we have hot summers as well as cold winters, figuring out what I could knit and wear in warm weather comes naturally to me. Headbands keep coming back up as a theme. Lacy and/ or skinny ones keep my hair in place—up off my neck—and help keep me cool. My second-favorite hot-weather knit is a T-shirt I knit in lace-weight silk. Most of the knitters I know would not consider knitting anything that large in such a fine yarn and small needle size. So I come back to headbands. Even the finest-weight headbands in this book are faster than a worsted-weight sweater.

At some point I also realized that headbands could be very useful in winter, too. You see, beanies are great if you plan to wear them all day, but more often than not, I want to keep my ears warm for an hour or two, and then I go back inside. So I only rarely wear toques. I would rather be cold for a little bit than end up with hat-hair for the day! A nice thick, wide headband solves this problem and doesn't give me hat-hair. I pop one on to take a thirty-minute walk around the neighborhood, and then I just whip it off and go on with my day—and no hair issues. If you have straight hair and you always wear it smoothly down, hats might work fine for you. But those of us who have curly hair and wear it in a high bun or ponytail, or who like to tease our hair to get volume at the roots, can't just mash our hair flat and expect it to look the same later.

The headband patterns I published online were hugely popular, so I guess I'm not alone in thinking that headbands are quite useful quick knits. I found creating this collection to be greatly entertaining, and I hope that you find the pieces just as entertaining to knit and useful to wear!

Using These Patterns

Gauge

Most of the headbands in this book are made by knitting a strip and then grafting the ends together to make a seamless round. Making a "proper" gauge swatch would usually mean casting on more stitches than are in the headband. After you do this, you will adjust your needle size to make what only amounts to a ¼ in. / ½ cm difference in the headband width, which really doesn't matter in the end anyway. Does this seem crazy to anyone else? I am a stickler for gauge when knitting a sweater because it *matters* if you want a sweater that fits. But if it doesn't matter, why take an extra step if it won't make your project better? So in light of this, for headbands knit as a strip to be joined, I do not list gauge in the conventional way, as so many stitches to a certain number of inches. Instead, I have indicated how wide the headband ought to be and where, after you have knit a certain length. The headband is the swatch. Should your headband not measure up, I would encourage you to look at it, feel it, and decide if you like it. If you do, feel free to proceed with just one warning: If your headband is significantly wider (by 1 in. / 3 cm or more), and your stitches loose, your headband might not have enough "spring" to stay on well, and you may want to tighten up.

Now, in contrast, in the case of the headbands that are knit in the round, you certainly can start the headband and then measure it to see if it will fit, but I think it is faster and easier in these cases to make a gauge swatch before starting the headband. Instructions for swatching are included in the pattern.

Needle Size

I wish I could list one needle size that would give each of you a perfect result, but I can't. Some knitters like to pull each stitch so it fits firmly around the needle, while others loop the stitches onto the needle so they sit very loosely. I am on the loose end of the spectrum, and I have a friend who uses needles six sizes larger than mine to end up with the same result. I am not exaggerating. If she is using US 11 (8 mm) needles, I use US 6 (4 mm) needles, and we end up with the same gauge. In this book, the needle size given is in the middle. If you know you work tighter or looser than average, you might want to start off swatching with a larger or smaller needle than listed. Thankfully, for most of the projects in this book, exact gauge and thus needle size are not vital. You can be a little bit off and have a successful project: one that fits and looks good.

If your headband is too small, use a larger needle size. If your headband is too large, use a smaller needle size.

Yarn

These patterns are perfect for trying out new yarns, using up leftovers from other projects, and otherwise substituting. The main thing is to check how thick the yarn is (yarn weight)—each pattern indicates what weights I recommend, usually a range. The second thing to think about is the fiber content. Yarns that are mostly acrylic, cotton, silk, linen, or alpaca may not be stretchy/springy enough to reliably stay on your head. If you just have to use a particular yarn, try a pattern where the headband is tied in the back. As it stretches out, you can tie the knot tighter and adjust the size. If you just have to use a certain pattern that is not tied, try making a size smaller, and if it still won't stay on, sew elastic thread through the backside to make it springy. Yarns that are mostly wool are ideal for headbands. Wool is very elastic, and the moisture and warmth from your body will revive it and keep it from getting stretched out. Nylon, polyester, and elastane (spandex) are often mixed with other fibers to give yarn more stretch. They can help to make cotton bouncy, so if you find cotton yarn mixed with any of these, pull the yarn to see if it has any stretch. If it does, don't worry about the cotton content.

Yarn weights, in order of thinnest to thickest

Name used in this book	CYCA standard weight number	Other names
Lace	0	Fingering
Fingering	1	Sock, Baby
Sport	2	Baby
DK	3	Light Worsted
Worsted	4	Aran
Aran	5	Bulky, Chunky
Bulky	6	Super Bulky

Head Sizes

If possible, measure the head you are knitting for. If you can't (perhaps you are knitting a gift and wish to surprise the recipient), err on the side of too small, except when working stranded knitting. Stranded colorwork has limited stretch, and it may not stretch enough if sized too small. Other than the stranded headbands, basically all the headbands in this book will fit acceptably on a head the next size larger.

Keep in mind that a six-year-old who seems to have a big head may very well have a head the same size as an adult. It happens more often than you might think, so it is always best to measure when possible.

The head sizes in this book are as follows:
Newborn: 13 in. / 33 cm to 15 in. / 38 cm
Baby: 15 in. / 38 cm to 17 in. / 43 cm
Toddler: 17 in. / 43 cm to 19 in. / 48 cm
Child: 19 in. / 48 cm to 21 in. / 53 cm
Adult SM: 21 in. / 53 cm to 23 in. / 58 cm
Adult LG: 23 in. / 58 cm to 25 in. / 63 cm

Knit-Purl
HEADBANDS

Garter

It doesn't get any easier than simple garter stitch! Instructions are given for all yarn weights so you can use *whatever* yarn you want. My choices include a crazy bulky T-shirt yarn, a medium-weight fuzzy yarn that reminds me of denim, and a sturdy lace-weight cotton-linen yarn.

Left to right: Samples C (Hooked Zpagetti Super Bulky), A (Schulana Mersilca Aran), and B (Diamond Pima Lino Lace)

Garter

SIZES

To fit everyone; just tie it larger or smaller. Note that the bulky yarns might make a very large knot on a small child's head! Lighter-weight yarns are recommended for children.

FINISHED MEASUREMENTS

Approximately 2 in. / 5 cm wide by 36 in. / 91 cm long

YARN

Sample A: Schulana Mersilca; Aran weight; 60% silk, 28% wool, 12% cashmere; 100 yd. / 92 m per .9 oz. / 25 g skein
   1 skein #203

Sample B: Diamond Pima Lino Lace; lace weight; 60% cotton, 40% linen; 465 yd. / 425 m per 1.7 oz. / 50 g skein
   1 skein #267

Sample C: Hoooked Zpagetti; super-bulky weight; 90% recycled cotton, 10% other fibers; 131 yd. / 120 m per 34 oz. / 975 g skein
   1 skein Coral (*Note:* This yarn also comes in much smaller skeins that would be more than enough for one head-band. I used a huge one because that is what my local yarn shop carries.)

YARN SUBSTITUTIONS

Try any yarn you want. Just check the pattern for how many stitches to cast on for your chosen yarn weight.

NEEDLES AND GAUGE

Needle size depends on yarn weight. Choose a size that makes a band 2 in. / 5 cm wide, measuring about 1 in. / 2.5 cm above the cast-on edge once you have knit about 2 in. / 5 cm.

    Lace: US 1 (2.25 mm)
    Fingering: US 3 (3.25 mm)
    Sport: US 5 (3.75 mm)
    DK: US 7 (4.5 mm)
    Worsted/Aran: US 9 (5.5 mm)
    Bulky: US 11 (8 mm)
    Super Bulky: US 17 (12.25 mm)

PATTERN NOTES

- This headband is a thin strip of garter stitch.
- To wear, wrap around your head, tie loosely, and then pull it off your head (to avoid tying your hair into the knot) and tighten up the knot.

STITCHES AND SKILLS

Knit (k)

PATTERN

Cast on a number of stitches according to your yarn weight, as follows:

    Lace: 16
    Fingering: 14
    Sport: 12
    DK: 10
    Worsted/Aran: 8
    Bulky: 6
    Super Bulky: 4

Row 1: Knit all stitches.
Repeat Row 1 until piece is 36 in. / 91.5 cm long.
Bind off.
Weave in yarn tails.

Wash the headband, and block it without pins.

Variation: Work until the band is 16–18 in. / 40.5–45.5 cm long and then graft or sew the ends together for a not-tied headband (shown in Zpagetti, to fit an adult).

1x1 Ribbed

The most basic of stitches (ribbing) sits a little flatter when you alternate ribbed rows with all-knit rows. Since this pattern is so simple, there are directions for every weight of yarn except lace. For the most perfect-looking edge possible, learn how to work a tubular cast-on and bind-off, though any cast-on/bind-off will work.

Top of stack to bottom: Samples A (Woolfolk Tynd Fingering), B (Noro Cyochin Worsted), and C (Malabrigo Rasta Super Bulky)

1x1 Ribbed

SIZES
Newborn (Baby, Toddler, Child, Adult SM, Adult LG)

FINISHED MEASUREMENTS
Circumference: 10 (12, 14, 16, 18, 20) in. / 25 (31, 36, 41, 46, 51) cm
Width: 2 (2½, 3, 3½, 4, 4) in. / 5 (6, 8, 9, 10, 10) cm

YARN
Sample A: Woolfolk Tynd; fingering weight; 100% Ovis XXI Ultimate Merino; 223 yd. / 205 m per 1.7 oz. / 50 g skein
    1 skein #9
Sample B: Noro Cyochin; worsted weight; 86% wool, 7% mohair, 7% silk; 196 yd. / 180 m per 3.5 oz. / 100 g skein
    1 skein #8
Sample C: Malabrigo Rasta; super-bulky weight; 100% merino wool; 90 yd. / 82 m per 5.3 oz. / 150 g skein
    1 skein #864 Porrinho

YARN SUBSTITUTIONS
Try any springy yarn. Multicolored, solid, or thick and thin will all work well. In the case of a not-so-stretchy yarn, like the Noro, try making the next size down or weaving elastic thread through the back side to keep it from stretching out.

NEEDLES AND GAUGE
Use needles for knitting in the round, as follows (or whatever size gets you the desired gauge):
    Fingering: US 1 (2.25 mm)
    Sport: US 3 (3.25 mm)
    DK: US 5 (3.75 mm)
    Worsted: US 7 (4.5 mm)
    Aran: US 9 (5.5 mm)
    Bulky: US 11 (8 mm)

Because this headband is worked in the round, it is faster to make a swatch than to cast on and restart if it is too large. To work a swatch, cast on 20 stitches and work in pattern stitch (Row 1: Knit all stitches; Row 2: [K1, p1] 10 times. Repeat [Rows 1–2] 15 times). The width of your swatch should measure as follows: Fingering, 3 in. / 8 cm; Sport, 3½ in. / 9 cm; DK, 3¾ in. / 9.5 cm); Worsted, 5 in. / 13 cm; Bulky, 6½ in. / 16 cm; Super Bulky, 11 in. / 28 cm.

PATTERN NOTES
• This headband is worked in the round.

STITCHES AND SKILLS
Knit (k), purl (p), and working in the round.

PATTERN

Cast on a number of stitches according to your yarn weight, as follows:

Fingering: 66 (80, 94, 106, 120, 132)
Sport: 56 (68, 80, 92, 102, 114)
DK: 54 (64, 74, 86, 96, 106)
Worsted: 40 (48, 56, 64, 72, 80)
Bulky: 30 (36, 42, 48, 54, 60)
Super Bulky: 18 (22, 26, 30, 32, 36)

Round 1: [K1, p1] around.
Round 2: Knit all stitches.
Repeat Rounds 1–2 until headband is 2 (2½, 3, 3½, 4, 4) in. /
5 (6, 8, 9, 10, 10) cm long.
Round 3: [K1, p1] around.
Bind off loosely.
Weave in yarn tails.

Wash the headband, and block it without pins.

1x1 Ribbed

Stitches

☐ k
⊡ p

▬ Repeat

I-Cord

I-cord is simple and fast to knit, and makes for a really easy and fun headband!

Top of stack to bottom: Samples A (HiKoo Kenzie Worsted), B (Istex Álafosslopi Bulky), and C (Lang Yarns Asia Fingering)

I-Cord

SIZES
To fit everyone; just tie it larger or smaller. Note that the bulky yarns might make a very large knot on a small child's head. Lighter-weight yarns are recommended for children.

FINISHED MEASUREMENTS
Length: 30 in. / 76 cm

YARN
Sample A: HiKoo Kenzie; worsted weight; 50% New Zealand merino, 25% nylon, 10% angora, 10% alpaca, 5% silk noils; 160 yd. / 146 m per 1.7 oz. / 50 g skein
    1 skein #1015 Boysenberry
Sample B: Istex Álafosslopi; bulky weight; 100% wool; 109 yd. / 100 m per 3.5 oz. / 100 g skein
    1 skein #7623 Neon Yellow
Sample C: Lang Yarns Asia; fingering weight; 70% silk, 30% yak; 160 yd. / 145 m per 1.7 oz. / 50 g skein
    1 skein color #14

YARN SUBSTITUTIONS
Try any yarn you want. Even hairy or eyelash yarns will work if you enjoy using them.

NEEDLES AND GAUGE

Use two double-pointed needles or a circular needle. Needle size depends on yarn weight, as follows:

Lace: US 1 (2.25 mm)
Fingering: US 3 (3.25 mm)
Sport: US 5 (3.75 mm)
DK: US 7 (4.5 mm)
Worsted/Aran: US 9 (5.5 mm)
Bulky: US 11 (8 mm)
Super Bulky: US 17 (12.25 mm)

Gauge is not critical for this headband.

PATTERN NOTES

- This headband is a long cord that is tied on.
- To wear, wrap it around your head and tie a loose knot. Pull it off gently (to avoid tying hair into the knot), and then tighten and straighten out the knot.

STITCHES AND SKILLS

Knit (k).

PATTERN

Cast on 3 stitches.

Row 1: Knit all stitches.
Row 2: Without turning the needle with the stitches on it, slide the 3 stitches to the other end of the needle, and then knit them. (You will be pulling the working yarn from the leftmost stitch on the needle, across the back of all stitches.)
Repeat Row 2 until the cord is 30 in. /76.2 cm long.
Bind off.
Weave in yarn tails.

Wash the headband, and block it without pins.

Shaped Garter Bulky

This headband is simple and warm—really, really warm. When you have an hour to knit, make one of these to keep your ears toasty in the freezing cold!

Left to right: Samples B (Malabrigo Rasta Bulky) and A (Lana Grossa Alta Moda Super Baby Bulky)

Shaped Garter Bulky

SIZES
Newborn (Baby, Toddler, Child, Adult SM, Adult LG) to fit heads 14 (16, 18, 20, 22, 24) in. / 35 (41, 46, 51, 56, 61) cm around

FINISHED MEASUREMENTS
Circumference: 12 (14, 16, 18, 20, 22) in. / 31 (36, 41, 46, 51, 56) cm, after knot is tied
Width in middle: 5 in. / 13 cm

YARN
Sample A: Lana Grossa Alta Moda Super Baby; bulky weight; 67% Wool, 30% Alpaca, 5% Nylon; 66 yd. / 60 m per 1.75 oz. / 50 g ball
   1 ball #7395 Cream
Sample B: Malabrigo Rasta; bulky weight; 100% merino wool; 90 yd. / 82 m per 5.3 oz. / 150 g skein
   1 skein #868 Coronilla

YARN SUBSTITUTIONS
Any bulky-weight yarn will work. Textures and crazy colors will work beautifully.

NEEDLES AND GAUGE
Use needles for knitting flat, US 15 (10 mm) or whatever size makes a band 5 in. / 12.7 cm wide, measuring 1 in. / 2.5 cm below the needle once you have knit about 12 in. / 30.5 cm.

PATTERN NOTES
• This is a rhombus-shaped headband that is tied on.
• To wear, wrap it around your head and tie a loose knot. Pull the scarf off gently (to avoid tying your hair into the knot), and then tighten and straighten out the knot.

STITCHES AND SKILLS
Knit (k), make one right (M1R), and knit two together (k2tog).

PATTERN

Cast on 2 stitches.

Rows 1–2: K2. (2 sts)
Row 3: K1, M1R, k1. (3 sts)
Row 4: K3.
Row 5: K2, M1R, k1. (4 sts)
Row 6: K4.
Row 7: K3, M1R, k1. (5 sts)
Rows 8–9: K5.
Repeat [Rows 8–9] 3 more times.
Row 10: K5.
Row 11: K4, M1R, k1. (6 sts)
Row 12: K6.
Row 13: K5, M1R, k1. (7 sts)
Row 14: K7.
Row 15: K6, M1R, k1. (8 sts)
Row 16: K8.
Row 17: K7, M1R, k1. (9 sts)
Row 18: K9.
Row 19: K8, M1R, k1. (10 sts)
Rows 20–21: K10.
Repeat Rows 20–21 until band
   is 8 (10, 12, 14, 16, 18) in. /
   20 (25, 30, 36, 41, 46) cm long.
Row 22 (WS): K10.
Row 23: K7, k2tog, k1. (9 sts)
Row 24: K9.
Row 25: K6, k2tog, k1. (8 sts)
Row 26: K8.
Row 27: K5, k2tog, k1. (7 sts)
Row 28: K7.
Row 29: K4, k2tog, k1. (6 sts)
Row 30: K6.
Row 31: K3, k2tog, k1. (5 sts)
Rows 32–33: K5.
Repeat [Rows 32–33] 3 more times.

Shaped Garter Bulky

Stitches	
☐ RS: k	━ Work 4 times
● WS: k	━ Repeat until band is
⊠ M1R	8 (10, 12, 14, 16, 18) in./
⧄ k2tog	20.5 (25.5, 30.5, 35.5, 40.5, 45.5) cm long

Row 34: K5.
Row 35: K2, k2tog, k1. (4 sts)
Row 36: K4.
Row 37: K1, k2tog, k1 (3 sts).
Row 38: K3.
Row 39: K1, k2tog. (2 sts)
Row 40: K2.
Bind off.
Weave in yarn tails.

Wash headband, and block it without pins.

Seeds

Basic seed stitch goes on bias with increases and decreases. Almost any skinny yarn will work well for this, but I made mine using a simple linen yarn and a unique "crepe" wool from Habu. *Note:* The crepe wool is a purposely overtwisted yarn—it has extra twist starched in and will be a little more twisty than the usual yarn. Don't let it get wet before knitting, or the twistiness will become worse. When you wash the headband, it will spring in a way quite unlike the usual balanced-twist yarn!

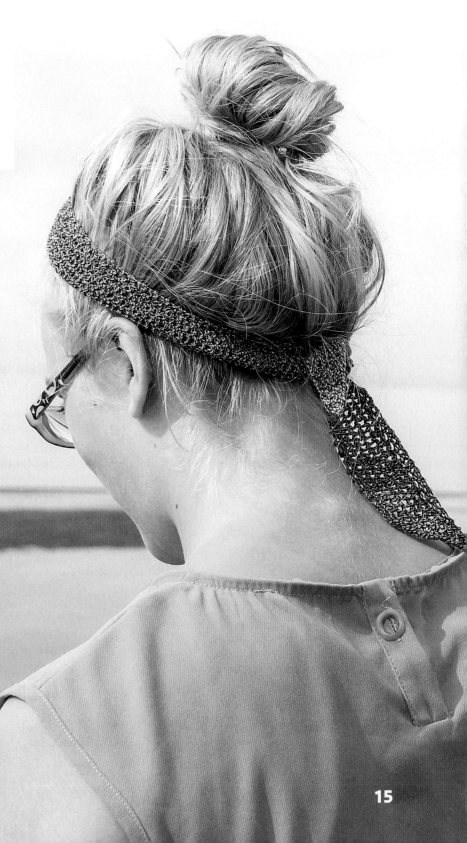

Left to right: Samples B (Louet Euroflax Sport) and A (Habu Textiles Wool Crepe N-90 Fingering)

Seeds

SIZES
To fit everyone (just tie it larger or smaller)

FINISHED MEASUREMENTS
Length: 30 in. / 76 cm
Width: 2 in. / 5 cm

YARN
Sample A: Habu Textiles Wool Crepe N-90; fingering weight; 100% wool; 125 yd. / 111 m per 1 oz. /2 8 g cone
    1 cone #4 Charcoal
Sample B: Louet Euroflax sport weight; 100% wet-spun linen; 270 yd. / 246 m per 3.5 oz. / 100 g skein
    1 skein #46 Cedarwood

YARN SUBSTITUTIONS
Try any fingering or sport-weight yarn. Colorful fun yarns and the simplest plain yarns all work equally well.

NEEDLES AND GAUGE
Use needles for knitting flat, US 5 (3.75 mm) or whatever size makes a headband 3 in. / 7.5 cm wide, measuring along the cast-on edge once you have knit about 2 in. / 5 cm. (*Note:* Once you have about 6 in. / 15 cm knit, you will see that the fabric biases, which make the ends pointy, and the band will end up thinner than 3 in. / 7.5 cm.)

PATTERN NOTES
• This headband is a long rectangle that is tied on.
• To wear it, wrap it around your head and tie a loose knot. Pull the scarf off gently (to avoid tying your hair into the knot), and then tighten and straighten out the knot.
• Work the edge stitches, including the increase and decrease, loosely.

STITCHES AND SKILLS
Knit (k), purl (p), make one right (M1R), knit two together (k2tog), and purl two together (p2tog).

PATTERN

Cast on 15 stitches.

Rows 1–2: K1, [p1, k1] 7 times.
Row 3: K1, k2tog, [p1, k1] 5 times, M1R, p1, k1.
Row 4: K1, p1, M1R, [p1, k1] 5 times, p2tog, k1.
Repeat Rows 3–4 until the band is 30 in. / 76 cm
   long, measuring along one side.
Rows 5–6: K1, [p1, k1] 7 times.
Bind off.
Weave in yarn tails.

Wash the headband, and block it without pins.

Seeds

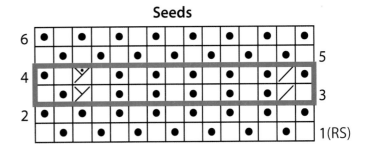

Stitches

☐ RS: k; WS: p	— Repeat until scarf is
● RS: p; WS: k	30 in. / 76 cm long
⧄ RS: M1R	
⧅ WS: M1R	
⧸ RS: k2tog; WS: p2tog	

I-Cord Garter

The next step up from plain garter stitch: Here we have shaping so the band fits neatly over your ears and around the back of your neck, with a tidy I-cord edge for a crisp, professional look. Besides looking good, I-cord stabilizes the edge and keeps the garter from stretching out, resulting in a fluffy garter headband that keeps you extra warm but won't stretch completely out of shape and fall off. This is perfect for alpaca-based, extra-soft but not springy yarns that otherwise might not stay on your head very well.

Left to right: Samples A (Shibui MAAI DK) and B (Yarn Ink Superwash DK)

I-Cord Garter

SIZES
Newborn (Baby, Toddler, Child, Adult SM, Adult LG) to fit heads 14 (16, 18, 20, 22, 24) in. / 35 (41, 46, 51, 56, 61) cm around

FINISHED MEASUREMENTS
Circumference: 10 (12, 14, 16, 18, 20) in. / 25 (31, 36, 41, 46, 51) cm

YARN
Sample A: Shibui MAAI; DK weight; 70% superbaby alpaca, 30% fine merino; 175 yd. / 160 m per 1.7 oz. / 50 g skein
   1 skein #2028 Trail
Sample B: Yarn Ink Superwash DK; DK weight; 100% super-wash merino wool; 200 yd. / 180 m per 4 oz. / 115 g skein
   1 skein Om

YARN SUBSTITUTIONS
Try any sport- to worsted-weight yarn with a bit of stretch—the fluffier, the better, in this case.

NEEDLES AND GAUGE

Use needles for knitting flat, US 6 (4 mm) or whatever size makes a headband 2 in. / 5 cm wide, measuring along the cast-on edge once you have knit about 2 in. / 5 cm.

PATTERN NOTES

• This is a shaped, round headband.

STITCHES AND SKILLS

Knit (k); make one right (M1R); slip stitch (sl); slip, slip, knit (ssk); provisional cast-on; and grafting.

PATTERN

Cast on 11 stitches using a provisional cast-on.

Rows 1–2: Sl 3, k8. (11 sts)
Repeat [Rows 1–2] 8 more times.
Row 3: Sl 3, k5, M1R, k3. (12 sts)
Row 4: Sl 3, k9.
Row 5: Sl 3, k6, M1R, k3. (13 sts)
Row 6: Sl 3, k10.
Row 7: Sl 3, k7, M1R, k3. (14 sts)
Row 8: Sl 3, k11.
Row 9: Sl 3, k8, M1R, k3. (15 sts)
Row 10: Sl 3, k12.
Row 11: Sl 3, k9, M1R, k3. (16 sts)
Row 12: Sl 3, k13.
Row 13: Sl 3, k10, M1R, k3. (17 sts)
Row 14: Sl 3, k14.
Row 15: Sl 3, k11, M1R, k3. (18 sts)
Row 16: Sl 3, k15.
Row 17: Sl 3, k12, M1R, k3. (19 sts)
Row 18: Sl 3, k16.
Row 19: Sl 3, k13, M1R, k3. (20 sts)
Row 20: Sl 3, k17.

Row 21: Sl 3, k14, M1R, k3. (21 sts)
Row 22: Sl 3, k18.
Rows 23–24: Sl 3, k18.
Repeat Rows 23–24 until band is 6 (8, 10, 12, 14, 16) in. / 15 (20.5, 25.5, 30.5, 35.5, 40.5) cm long.
Row 25: Sl 3, k13, ssk, k3. (20 sts)
Row 26: Sl 3, k17.
Row 27: Sl 3, k12, ssk, k3. (19 sts)
Row 28: Sl 3, k16.
Row 29: Sl 3, k11, ssk, k3. (18 sts)
Row 30: Sl 3, k15.
Row 31: Sl 3, k10, ssk, k3. (17 sts)
Row 32: Sl 3, k14.
Row 33: Sl 3, k9, ssk, k3. (16 sts)
Row 34: Sl 3, k13.
Row 35: Sl 3, k8, ssk, k3. (15 sts)
Row 36: Sl 3, k12.
Row 37: Sl 3, k7, ssk, k3. (14 sts)
Row 38: Sl 3, k11.
Row 39: Sl 3, k6, ssk, k3. (13 sts)
Row 40: Sl 3, k10.
Row 41: Sl 3, k5, ssk, k3. (12 sts)
Row 42: Sl 3, k9.
Row 43: Sl 3, k4, ssk, k3. (11 sts)
Row 44: Sl 3, k8.
Rows 45–46: Sl 3, k8.
Repeat [Rows 45–46] 8 more times.
Do not bind off. Undo the provisional cast-on, place those stitches on a needle, and then graft the ends of the headband together.
Weave in yarn tails.

Wash the headband, and block it without pins.

Stitches	
▨ No stitch	— Work 9 times
☐ RS: k	— Repeat until band is
⊡ WS: k	6 (8, 10, 12, 14, 16) in./
⊻ RS: sl 1	15 (20.5, 25.5, 30.5, 33.5, 40.5) cm long
⊽ WS: sl 1	
⊠ M1R	
◩ ssk	

I-Cord Garter

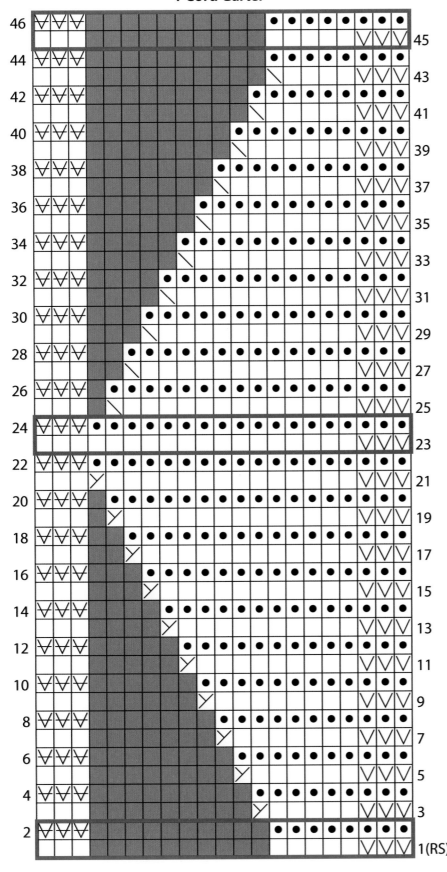

Waves

To make this headband warmer, I adapted a lace stitch to remove the holes. The pattern stitch is not intuitive, so count carefully, follow the directions exactly, and when you have it half-knit, you will see the pattern emerge. Up to that point, it will look strange; it doesn't "make sense" as you work it.

Top to bottom: Samples B (Lion Brand Amazing Worsted) and A (Knit Picks Reverie Worsted)

Waves

SIZES

Adult SM (Adult LG) to fit heads 22 (24) in. / 56 (61) cm around

FINISHED MEASUREMENTS

Circumference: 16½ (18) in. / 42 (46) cm
Width: 4 in. / 10 cm

YARN

Sample A: Knit Picks Reverie; worsted weight; 80% baby alpaca, 20% acrylic; 137 yd. / 125 m per 1.7 oz. / 50 g skein

   1 skein #26114 Gemstone

Sample B: Lion Brand Amazing; worsted weight; 53% wool, 47% acrylic; 147 yd. / 135 m per 1.7 oz. / 50 g skein

   1 skein #208 Aurora

YARN SUBSTITUTIONS

This stitch pattern looks best in single ply or other yarns with indistinct plies. Use worsted weight or any other yarn that will work up to the same gauge. Because this type of yarn tends to stretch out, the headband has a fair amount of negative ease so it will stay on.

NEEDLES AND GAUGE

Use needles for knitting in the round, US 7 (4.5 mm), or whatever size gets you gauge. Because this headband is worked in the round, it is faster to make a swatch than to cast on and restart if it is not the right size. Cast on 15 stitches and work flat (back and forth) from the chart with no repeats. Odd-numbered rows are right side, even are wrong side in the swatch (headband is worked in the round). Your swatch should be just over 3 in. / 7.5 cm wide in the middle after it is knit.

PATTERN NOTES

• This headband is worked in the round.

STITCHES AND SKILLS

Knit (k); purl (p); knit and purl in one stitch [(k, p) in 1]; purl and knit in one stitch [(p, k) in 1]; knit, purl, knit in one stitch [(k, p, k) in 1]; knit two together (k2tog); slip, slip, knit (ssk); knit three together (k3tog); and working in the round.

PATTERN

Cast on 78 (85) stitches and join in the round, being careful not to twist the stitches.

Rounds 1–4: P1, [k2, p2, k2, p1] 11 (12) times.
Round 5: (K, p) in 1, [k2, p2, k2, (k, p, k) in 1] 11 (12) times. (101 [110] sts)
Round 6: [K4, p2, k3] 11 (12) times, k2.
Round 7: K1, (k, p) in 1, k2, [ssk, k2tog, k2, (k, p, k) in 1, k2] 10 (11) times, ssk, k2tog, k2, (p, k) in 1.
Round 8: K101 (110).
Round 9: (K, p) in 1, k2, ssk, [k2tog, k2, (k, p, k) in 1, k2, ssk] 10 (11) times, k2tog, k2, (p, k) in 1, k1.
Round 10: K101 (110).
Round 11: K1, (k, p) in 1, k2, [ssk, k2tog, k2, (k, p, k) in 1, k2] 10 (11) times, ssk, k2tog, k2, (p, k) in 1.
Round 12: K101 (110).
Round 13: (K, p) in 1, k2, ssk, [k2tog, k2, (k, p, k) in 1, k2, ssk] 10 (11) times, k2tog, k2, (p, k) in 1, k1.
Repeat [Rounds 10–13] 2 more times.
Round 14: K101 (110).
Round 15: K1, (k, p) in 1, k2, [ssk, k2tog, k2, (k, p, k) in 1, k2] 10 (11) times, ssk, k2tog, k2, (p, k) in 1.
Round 16: P1, k1, [k8, p1] 11 (12) times.
Round 17: P1, k2, ssk, [k2tog, k2, p1, k2, ssk] 10 (11) times, k3tog, k2, p1. (78 [85] sts)
Rounds 18–21: P1, [k2, p2, k2, p1] 11 (12) times.
Bind off loosely.
Weave in yarn tails.

Wash the headband, and block it without pins.

Waves

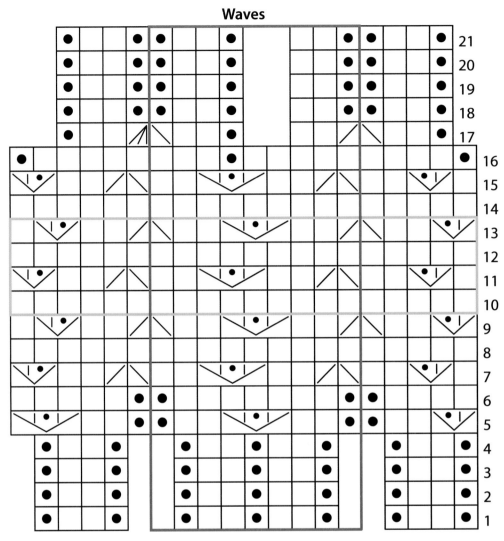

Stitches

☐ k

⊡ p

◹ (k, p) in 1

◺ (p, k) in 1

▱ (k, p, k) in 1

◿ k2tog

◺ ssk

⧄ k3tog

— Work 3 times up

— Work 10 (11) times

Cabled
HEADBANDS

Simple Cable

If you are new to cables, try this one first! In bulky weight, it works up quickly, and it uses the easiest cable of all.

Top to bottom: Samples B (Knit Picks The Big Cozy Bulky) and A (Lion Brand Alpine Wool Tweed Bulky)

Simple Cable

SIZES
Newborn (Baby, Toddler, Child, Adult SM, Adult LG) to fit heads 14 (16, 18, 20, 22, 24) in. / 35 (41, 46, 51, 56, 61) cm around

FINISHED MEASUREMENTS
Circumference: 11 (13, 15, 17, 19, 21) in. / 28 (33, 38, 43, 48, 53) cm

YARN
Sample A: Lion Brand Alpine Wool Tweed; bulky weight; 77% wool, 15% acrylic, 8% rayon; 93 yd. / 85 m per 3 oz. / 85 g skein
　　1 skein #223 Oatmeal
Sample B: Knit Picks The Big Cozy; bulky weight; 55% superfine alpaca, 45% Peruvian highland wool; 44 yd. / 40 m per 3.5 oz. / 100 g skein
　　1 skein #26489 Garnet Heather

YARN SUBSTITUTIONS
Try a smooth worsted-, Aran-, or bulky-weight yarn.

NEEDLES AND GAUGE

Use needles for knitting flat, US 13 (9 mm) or whatever size makes a band 2½ in. / 6 cm wide, measuring 1 in. / 2.5 cm below the needle once you have knit 4 in. / 10 cm.

PATTERN NOTES

• This headband is grafted together after knitting.

STITCHES AND SKILLS

Knit (k), purl (p), slip stitch (sl), cables (2/2 RC), provisional cast-on, and grafting.

PATTERN

Cast on 8 stitches using a provisional cast-on.

Row 1: K1, p1, k4, p1, k1.
Row 2: Sl 1 wyif, k1, p4, k1, p1.
Row 3: Sl 1, p1, 2/2 RC, p1, k1.
Row 4: Sl 1 wyif, k1, p4, k1, p1.
Row 5: Sl 1, p1, k4, p1, k1.
Row 6: Sl 1 wyif, k1, p4, k1, p1.
Row 7: Sl 1, p1, 2/2 RC, p1, k1.
Repeat Rows 4–7 until band is 11 (13, 15, 17, 19, 21) in. / 28 (33, 38, 43, 48, 53) cm long.
Do not bind off. Pull out provisional cast-on, place those stitches on a needle, and then graft the ends together.
Weave in yarn tails.

Wash the headband, and block it without pins.

Stitches

☐	RS: k; WS: p
●	RS: p; WS: k
Ⅴ	RS: sl 1; WS: sl 1 wyif
⟋⟍	2/2 RC

— Repeat until band is 11 (13, 15, 17, 19, 21) in./ 28 (33, 38, 43, 48, 53) cm long

Simple Cable

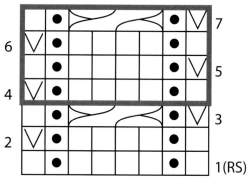

Braid

Cables on alternating sides make a braid.
If you can cable, you can make this braid!

Top to bottom: Samples A (Filatura di Crosa Zara Chiné DK) and B (KPC Cashmere 4 Ply Fingering)

Braid

SIZES
Newborn (Baby, Toddler, Child, Adult SM, Adult LG) to fit heads 14 (16, 18, 20, 22, 24) in. / 35 (41, 46, 51, 56, 61) cm around

FINISHED MEASUREMENTS
Circumference: 11 (13, 15, 17, 19, 21) in. / 28 (33, 38, 43, 48, 53) cm

YARN
Sample A: Filatura di Crosa Zara Chiné; DK weight; 100% superwash merino; 136 yd. / 125 m per 1.7 oz. / 50 g skein
   1 skein #824 Onyx
Sample B: KPC Cashmere 4 Ply; fingering weight; 100% cashmere; 95 yd. / 87 m per .9 oz. / 25 g skein
   1 skein Derby Grey

YARN SUBSTITUTIONS
Try any stretchy and smooth fingering-, sport-, or DK-weight yarn. (Use the needle size specified on the ball band of the yarn you choose.)

NEEDLES AND GAUGE
Use needles for knitting flat, as follows:
Fingering: US 2 (2.75 mm) for a 2 in. / 5 cm wide band, measuring 1 in. / 2.5 cm below the needle once you have knit 4 in. / 10 cm.
Sport: US 3 (3.25 mm) for a 2¼ in. / 5.5 cm wide band, measuring 1 in. / 2.5 cm below the needle once you have knit 4 in. / 10 cm.
DK: US 4 (3.5 mm) for a 2½ in. / 6 cm wide band, measuring 1 in. / 2.5 cm below the needle once you have knit 4 in. / 10 cm.

PATTERN NOTES
• This headband is grafted together after knitting.

STITCHES AND SKILLS
Knit (k), purl (p), cables (3/3 LC, 3/3 RC), provisional cast-on, and grafting.

PATTERN

Cast on 13 stitches using a provisional cast-on.

Row 1: K13.
Row 2: K2, p9, k2.
Row 3: K2, 3/3 LC, k5.
Row 4: K2, p9, k2.
Row 5: K13.
Row 6: K2, p9, k2.
Row 7: K5, 3/3 RC, k2.
Row 8: K2, p9, k2.
Row 9: K13.
Row 10: K2, p9, k2.
Row 11: K2, 3/3 LC, k5.

Row 12: K2, p9, k2.
Row 13: K13.
Row 14: K2, p9, k2.
Repeat Rows 7–14 until band is 11 (13, 15, 17, 19, 21) in. /
 28 (33, 38, 43, 48, 53) cm long, stopping when/if one
 more repeat will make the band too long. Leave it a little
 short instead.
Row 15: K5, 3/3 RC, k2.
Do not bind off. Undo your provisional cast-on, pick up
 those stitches, and then graft them to the other end.
Weave in yarn tails.

Wash the headband, and block it without pins.

Braid

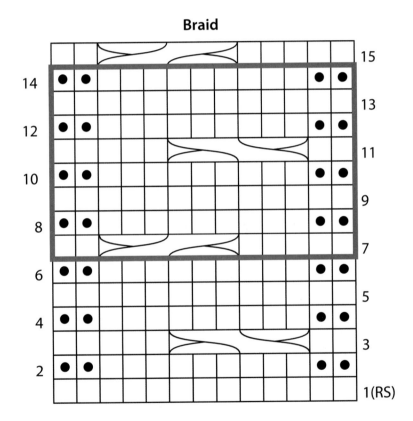

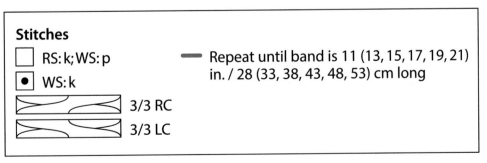

Stitches

☐ RS: k; WS: p

⦿ WS: k

▱ 3/3 RC

▱ 3/3 LC

— Repeat until band is 11 (13, 15, 17, 19, 21)
 in. / 28 (33, 38, 43, 48, 53) cm long

X&O Cables

Wrap someone you love in Xs and Os! I used a rustic, woolen spun yarn and a smooth, worsted spun yarn. Each makes nice, plump cables but gives a totally different effect.

Top to bottom: Samples B (Sweet Fiber Canadian Aran) and A (RainCityKnits Worsted)

X & O Cables

SIZES
Newborn (Baby, Toddler, Child, Adult SM, Adult LG) to fit heads 14 (16, 18, 20, 22, 24) in. / 35 (41, 46, 51, 56, 61) cm around

FINISHED MEASUREMENTS
Circumference: 11 (13, 15, 17, 19, 21) in. / 28 (33, 38, 43, 48, 53) cm

YARN
Sample A: RainCityKnits; worsted weight; 100% superwash merino; 218 yd. / 200 m per 3.5 oz. / 100 g skein
   1 skein Vermillion
Sample B: Sweet Fiber Canadian; Aran weight; 100% Canadian wool; 190 yd. / 208 m per 3.5 oz. / 100 g skein
   1 skein Breakwater

YARN SUBSTITUTIONS
Try a stretchy and smooth DK-, worsted-, or Aran-weight yarn. (Try a US 5 [3.75 mm] needle for DK weight, a US 7 [4.5 mm] for Aran, or start with the needle size specified on the ball band of the yarn you choose.)

NEEDLES AND GAUGE

Use needles for knitting flat, US 6 (4.0 mm) or whatever size makes a band 3.5 in. / 9 cm wide, measuring 1 in. / 3 cm below the needle once you have knit 3 in. / 7.5 cm.

PATTERN NOTES

• This headband is grafted together after knitting.

STITCHES AND SKILLS

Knit (k), purl (p), cables (2/2 RC, 2/2 LC), provisional cast-on, and grafting.

PATTERN

Cast on 16 stitches using a provisional cast-on.

Row 1: K3, p1, k8, p1, k3.
Row 2: K4, p8, k4.
Row 3: K3, p1, 2/2 RC, 2/2 LC, p1, k3.
Row 4: K4, p8, k4.
Row 5: K3, p1, k8, p1, k3.
Row 6: K4, p8, k4.
Row 7: K3, p1, 2/2 LC, 2/2 RC, p1, k3.
Row 8: K4, p8, k4.
Rows 9–12: Repeat Rows 5–8.
Row 13: K3, p1, k8, p1, k3.
Row 14: K4, p8, k4.
Row 15: K3, p1, 2/2 RC, 2/2 LC, p1, k3.
Row 16: K4, p8, k4.
Repeat Rows 1–16 until band is 11 (13, 15, 17, 19, 21) in. / 28 (33, 38, 43, 48, 53) cm long, ending on Row 15. If one more repeat will make the band too long, don't work it; let it be short instead.
Do not bind off. Pull out the provisional cast-on, place those stitches on a needle, and graft the ends of the band together.
Weave in yarn tails.

Wash the headband, and block it without pins.

X & O Cables

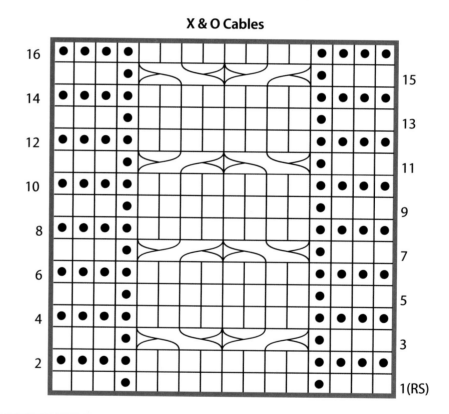

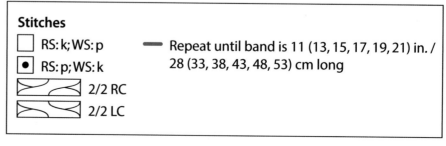

Stitches

☐ RS: k; WS: p

● RS: p; WS: k

▱ 2/2 RC

▱ 2/2 LC

— Repeat until band is 11 (13, 15, 17, 19, 21) in. / 28 (33, 38, 43, 48, 53) cm long

Round About

Simple cables make a playful circular pattern. This pattern is very flexible about the yarn weight used: Make it skinnier with a thinner yarn, or make a wide and bold band with heavier yarn.

Top to bottom: Samples A (Knit Picks Capra DK) and B (Schachenmayr Original Boston Super Bulky)

Round About

SIZES
Newborn (Baby, Toddler, Child, Adult SM, Adult LG) to fit heads 14 (16, 18, 20, 22, 24) in. / 35 (41, 46, 51, 56, 61) cm around

FINISHED MEASUREMENTS
Circumference: 12 (14, 16, 18, 20, 22) in. / 31 (36, 41, 46, 51, 56) cm

YARN
Sample A: Knit Picks Capra; DK weight; 85% merino, 15% cashmere; 123 yd. / 112 m per 1.75 oz. / 50 g skein
   1 skein #24963 Caviar
Sample B: Schachenmayr Original Boston; super-bulky weight; 70% acrylic, 30% wool; 60 yd. / 55 m per 1.7 oz. / 50 g skein
   1 skein #136 Neon Pink

YARN SUBSTITUTIONS
Try any stretchy and smooth DK-, worsted-, Aran-, or bulky-weight yarn and the appropriate needle size.

NEEDLES AND GAUGE

Use needles for knitting flat, as follows:

DK: US 7 (4.5 mm) or whatever size makes a band 2 in. / 5 cm wide, measuring 1 in. / 2.5 cm below the needle once you have knit about 3 in. / 7.5 cm.

Super Bulky: US 10 (6 mm), or whatever size makes a band 3.5 in. / 9 cm wide, measuring 1 in. / 2.5 cm below the needle once you have knit about 3 in. / 7.5 cm.

PATTERN NOTES

• This headband is grafted together after knitting.

STITCHES AND SKILLS

Knit (k), purl (p), slip stitch (sl), cables (3/2 LC, 3/2 RC, 3/3 RC), provisional cast-on, and grafting.

PATTERN

Cast on 16 stitches using a provisional cast-on.

Row 1: Sl 1, k15.
Row 2: Sl 1, k2, p10, k2, p1.
Rows 3–4: Repeat Rows 1–2.
Row 5: Sl 1, k2, 3/2 LC, 3/2 RC, k3.
Row 6: Sl 1, k2, p10, k2, p1.
Row 7: Sl 1, k4, 3/3 RC, k5.
Row 8: Sl 1, k2, p10, k2, p1.
Row 9: Sl 1, k2, 3/2 RC, 3/2 LC, k3.
Row 10: Sl 1, k2, p10, k2, p1.
Row 11: Sl 1, k15.
Row 12: Sl 1, k2, p10, k2, p1.
Rows 13–16: Repeat [Rows 11–12] 2 times.
Row 17: Sl 1, k2, 3/2 LC, 3/2 RC, k3.
Row 18: Sl 1, k2, p10, k2, p1.
Row 19: Sl 1, k4, 3/3 RC, k5.
Row 20: Sl 1, k2, p10, k2, p1.
Row 21: Sl 1, k2, 3/2 RC, 3/2 LC, k3.
Repeat Rows 10–21 until the band is 12 (14, 16, 18, 20, 22) in. / 31 (36, 41, 46, 51, 56) cm long. If one more repeat will make the band too long, stop knitting and let it be a little short instead.
Row 22: Sl 1, k2, p10, k2, p1.
Row 23: Sl 1, k15.
Do not bind off. Undo your provisional cast-on, pick up those stitches, and then graft them to the other end.
Weave in yarn tails.

Wash the headband, and block it without pins.

Round About

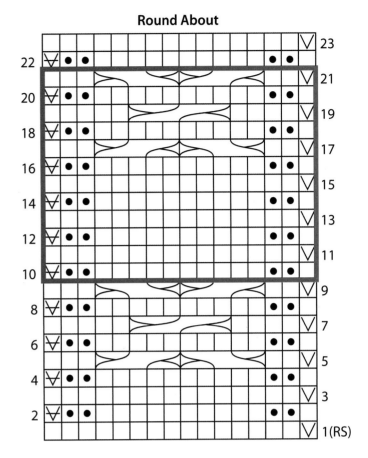

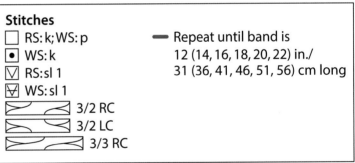

Stitches

☐ RS: k; WS: p	
• WS: k	
⋁ RS: sl 1	
⋀ WS: sl 1	
⟋⟍ 3/2 RC	
⟍⟋ 3/2 LC	
⟋⟍ 3/3 RC	

— Repeat until band is 12 (14, 16, 18, 20, 22) in./ 31 (36, 41, 46, 51, 56) cm long

Bamboo Cables

These cables don't look exactly like bamboo, but they remind me of it. They have a nice amount of stretch to them and are fun to knit as well.

40

Left to right: Samples A (RainCityKnits High Twist DK) and B (Malabrigo Merino Worsted)

Bamboo Cables

SIZES

Newborn (Baby, Toddler, Child, Adult SM, Adult LG) to fit heads 14 (16, 18, 20, 22, 24) in. / 35 (41, 46, 51, 56, 61) cm around

FINISHED MEASUREMENTS

Circumference: 11 (13, 15, 17, 19, 21) in. / 28 (33, 38, 43, 48, 53) cm

YARN

Sample A: RainCityKnits High Twist DK; DK weight; 100% superwash merino; 230 yd. / 210 m per 3.5 oz. / 100 g skein
   1 skein Bright Aqua
Sample B: Malabrigo Merino Worsted; worsted weight; 100% merino wool; 210 yd. / 195 m per 3.5 oz. / 100 g skein
   1 skein #23 Pagoda

YARN SUBSTITUTIONS

Try a stretchy and smooth DK-, worsted-, or Aran-weight yarn. (Start with a US 5 [3.75 mm] needle for DK weight and a US 8 [5 mm] for Aran, or use the needle size specified on the ball band of the yarn you choose and swatch as given in "Needles and Gauge.")

NEEDLES AND GAUGE

Use needles for knitting flat, US 6 (4.0 mm), or whatever size makes a band 3.5 in. / 9 cm wide, measuring 1 in. / 2.5 cm below the needle once you have knit 4 in. / 10 cm.

PATTERN NOTES

• This headband is grafted together after knitting.

STITCHES AND SKILLS

Knit (k), purl (p), slip stitch (sl), cables (1/2 RC, 1/2 LC), provisional cast-on, and grafting.

PATTERN

Cast on 20 stitches using a provisional cast-on.

Row 1: Sl 1, p2, [k6, p2] twice, k1.
Row 2: Sl 1, k2, [p6, k2] twice, p1.
Row 3: Sl 1, p2, k6, p2, 1/2 RC, 1/2 LC, p2, k1.
Row 4: Sl 1, k2, [p6, k2] twice, p1.
Rows 5–8: Repeat Rows 3–4 twice.
Row 9: Sl 1, p2, [k6, p2] twice, k1.
Row 10: Sl 1, k2, [p6, k2] twice, p1.
Row 11: Sl 1, p2, 1/2 RC, 1/2 LC, p2, k6, p2, k1.
Row 12: Sl 1, k2, [p6, k2] twice, p1.

Rows 13–16: Repeat Rows 11–12 twice.

Repeat Rows 1–16 until band is 11 (13, 15, 17, 19, 21) in. / 28 (33, 38, 43, 48, 53) cm long. If one more repeat will make the band too long, stop knitting and let it be a little short instead.

Do not bind off. Undo your provisional cast-on, pick up those stitches, and then graft them to the other end.

Weave in yarn tails.

Wash the headband, and block it without pins.

Bamboo Cables

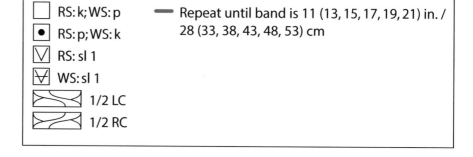

Stitches

☐	RS: k; WS: p
•	RS: p; WS: k
⋁	RS: sl 1
⋈	WS: sl 1
⟋	1/2 LC
⟍	1/2 RC

— Repeat until band is 11 (13, 15, 17, 19, 21) in. / 28 (33, 38, 43, 48, 53) cm

Labyrinth

Tiny one-stitch cables dance over the purl backdrop. In a soft gray, the look is elegant and subdued. In neon yellow, it is playful and attention grabbing.

Left to right: Samples B (Knit Picks Stroll Brights Fingering) and A (Patons Kroy Socks Fingering)

Labyrinth

SIZES
To fit a Child (Adult SM, Adult LG) or heads 19–21 (21–22, 22–24) in. / 48–53 (53–56, 56–61) cm around

FINISHED MEASUREMENTS
Circumference: 16½ (18, 19½) in. / 42 (46, 50) cm
    Width: 3½ in. / 9 cm

YARN
Sample A: Patons Kroy Socks; fingering weight; 75% washable wool, 25% nylon; 166 yd. / 152 m per 1.7 oz. / 50 g skein
    1 skein Flax

Sample B: Knit Picks Stroll Brights; fingering weight; 75% superwash merino wool, 25% nylon; 231 yd. / 210 m per 1.7 oz. / 50 g skein
    1 skein Pickle Juice #26403

YARN SUBSTITUTIONS
Try any springy, stretchy, fingering-weight yarn. Multicolor yarns may obscure the cables; solid or heathered colors will make them pop!

NEEDLES AND GAUGE
Use needles for knitting in the round, US 2 (2.75 mm), or whatever size gets you gauge. Because this headband is worked in the round, it is faster to make a swatch than to cast on and restart if it is not the right size. Cast on 24 stitches and work from the chart, going back and forth rather than in the round. Once your swatch is 3 in. / 8 cm long, measure about 1 in. / 2.5 cm above the cast-on edge, where it should be 3 in. / 7.5 cm wide.

PATTERN NOTES
• This headband is worked in the round.

STITCHES AND SKILLS
Knit (k), purl (p), cables (1/1 RC, 1/1 RPC, 1/1 LC, 1/1 LPC), and working in the round.

PATTERN

Cast on 132 (144, 156) stitches and join in the round, making sure that you don't let a twist in.

Work Rounds 1–31, following the chart on page 46 or the written instructions below.

Round 1: K1, p3, k1, p1, [p1, k1, p3, k2, p3, k1, p1] 10 (11, 12) times, p1, k1, p3, k1.
Round 2: 1/1 LPC, p2, 1/1 LPC, [1/1 RPC, p2, 1/1 RPC, 1/1 LPC, p2, 1/1 LPC] 10 (11, 12) times, 1/1 RPC, p2, 1/1 RPC.
Round 3: P1, k1, p3, k1, [k1, p3, k1, p2, k1, p3, k1] 10 (11, 12) times, k1, p3, k1, p1.
Round 4: P1, k1, p3, [1/1 LC, p3, k1, p2, k1, p3] 10 (11, 12) times, 1/1 LC, p3, k1, p1.
Round 5: P1, k1, p3, k1, [k1, p3, k1, p2, k1, p3, k1] 10 (11, 12) times, k1, p3, k1, p1.
Round 6: 1/1 RPC, p2, 1/1 RPC, [1/1 LPC, p2, 1/1 LPC, 1/1 RPC, p2, 1/1 RPC] 10 (11, 12) times, 1/1 LPC, p2, 1/1 LPC.
Round 7: K1, p3, k1, p1, [p1, k1, p3, k2, p3, k1, p1] 10 (11, 12) times, p1, k1, p3, k1.
Round 8: K1, p3, k1, p1, [p1, k1, p3, 1/1 LC, p3, k1, p1] 10 (11, 12) times, p1, k1, p3, k1.
Round 9: K1, p3, k1, p1, [p1, k1, p3, k2, p3, k1, p1] 10 (11, 12) times, p1, k1, p3, k1.
Round 10: 1/1 LPC, p2, 1/1 LPC, [1/1 RPC, p2, 1/1 RPC, 1/1 LPC, p2, 1/1 LPC] 10 (11, 12) times, 1/1 RPC, p2, 1/1 RPC.
Round 11: P1, k1, p3, k1, [k1, p3, k1, p2, k1, p3, k1] 10 (11, 12) times, k1, p3, k1, p1.
Round 12: P1, 1/1 LPC, p2, [1/1 LC, p2, 1/1 RPC, p2, 1/1 LPC, p2] 10 (11, 12) times, 1/1 LC, p2, 1/1 RPC, p1.
Round 13: P2, k1, p2, k1, [k1, p2, k1, p4, k1, p2, k1] 10 (11, 12) times, k1, p2, k1, p2.
Round 14: P2, 1/1 LPC, 1/1 RPC, [1/1 LPC, 1/1 RPC, p4, 1/1 LPC, 1/1 RPC] 10 (11, 12) times, 1/1 LPC, 1/1 RPC, p2.
Round 15: P3, k2, p1, [p1, k2, p6, k2, p1] 10 (11, 12) times, p1, k2, p3.
Round 16: P3, 1/1 RC, p1, [p1, 1/1 RC, p6, 1/1 RC, p1] 10 (11, 12) times, p1, 1/1 RC, p3.
Round 17: P3, k2, p1, [p1, k2, p6, k2, p1] 10 (11, 12) times, p1, k2, p3.
Round 18: P2, 1/1 RPC, 1/1 LPC, [1/1 RPC, 1/1 LPC, p4, 1/1 RPC, 1/1 LPC] 10 (11, 12) times, 1/1 RPC, 1/1 LPC, p2.
Round 19: P2, k1, p2, k1, [k1, p2, k1, p4, k1, p2, k1] 10 (11, 12) times, k1, p2, k1, p2.
Round 20: P1, 1/1 RPC, p2, [1/1 LC, p2, 1/1 LPC, p2, 1/1 RPC, p2] 10 (11, 12) times, 1/1 LC, p2, 1/1 LPC, p1.
Round 21: P1, k1, p3, k1, [k1, p3, k1, p2, k1, p3, k1] 10 (11, 12) times, k1, p3, k1, p1.
Round 22: 1/1 RPC, p2, 1/1 RPC, [1/1 LPC, p2, 1/1 LPC, 1/1 RPC, p2, 1/1 RPC] 10 (11, 12) times, 1/1 LPC, p2, 1/1 LPC.

Round 23: K1, p3, k1, p1, [p1, k1, p3, k2, p3, k1, p1] 10 (11, 12) times, p1, k1, p3, k1.
Round 24: K1, p3, k1, p1, [p1, k1, p3, 1/1 LC, p3, k1, p1] 10 (11, 12) times, p1, k1, p3, k1.
Round 25: K1, p3, k1, p1, [p1, k1, p3, k2, p3, k1, p1] 10 (11, 12) times, p1, k1, p3, k1.
Round 26: 1/1 LPC, p2, 1/1 LPC, [1/1 RPC, p2, 1/1 RPC, 1/1 LPC, p2, 1/1 LPC] 10 (11, 12) times, 1/1 RPC, p2, 1/1 RPC.
Round 27: P1, k1, p3, k1, [k1, p3, k1, p2, k1, p3, k1] 10 (11, 12) times, k1, p3, k1, p1.
Round 28: P1, k1, p3, [1/1 LC, p3, k1, p2, k1, p3] 10 (11, 12) times, 1/1 LC, p3, k1, p1.
Round 29: P1, k1, p3, k1, [k1, p3, k1, p2, k1, p3, k1] 10 (11, 12) times, k1, p3, k1, p1.
Round 30: 1/1 RPC, p2, 1/1 RPC, [1/1 LPC, p2, 1/1 LPC, 1/1 RPC, p2, 1/1 RPC] 10 (11, 12) times, 1/1 LPC, p2, 1/1 LPC.
Round 31: K1, p3, k1, p1, [p1, k1, p3, k2, p3, k1, p1] 10 (11, 12) times, p1, k1, p3, k1.

Bind off.
Weave in yarn tails.

Wash the headband, and block it without pins.

Labyrinth

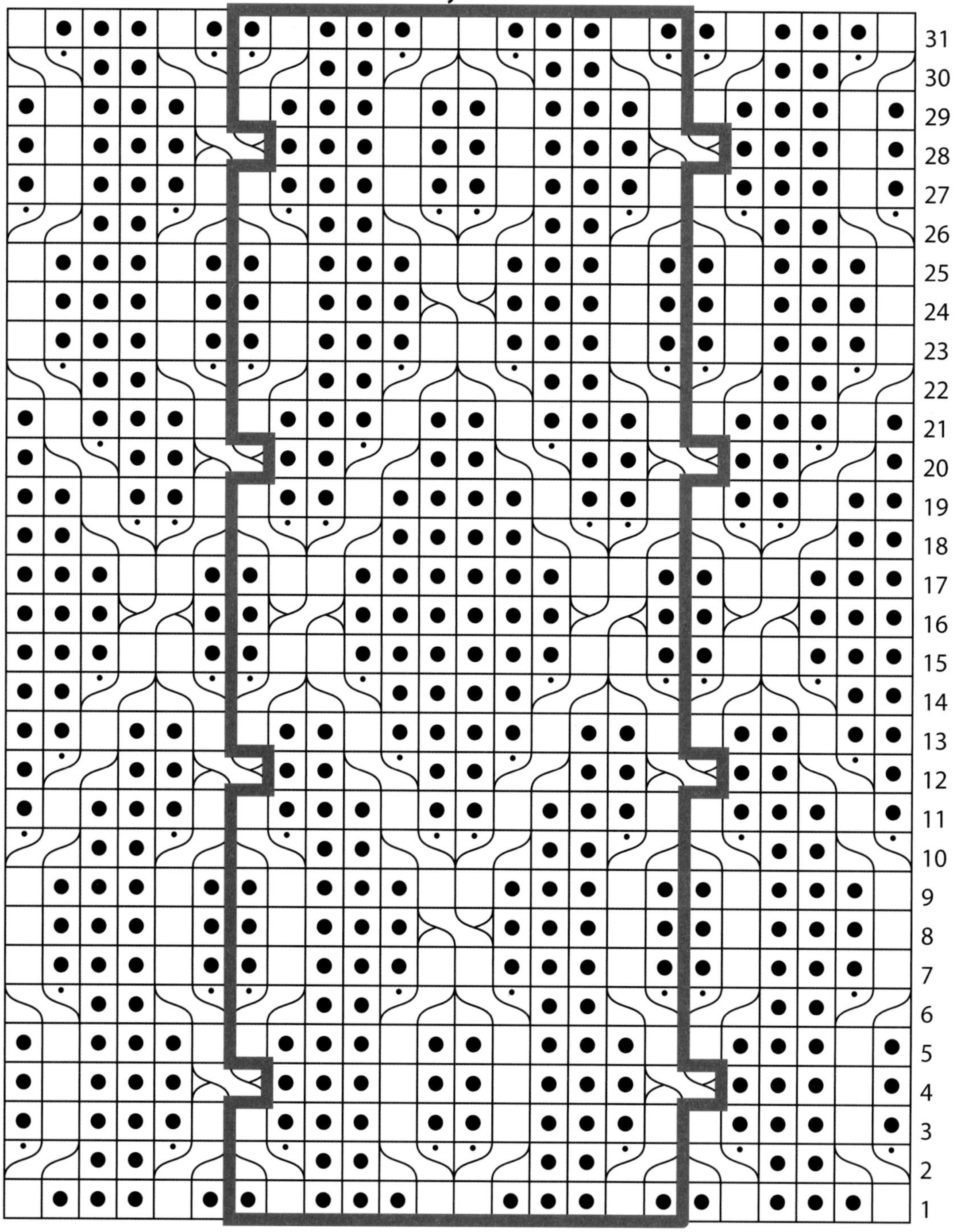

Stitches

- k
- p
- 1/1 RC
- 1/1 RPC
- 1/1 LC
- 1/1 LPC

Work 10 (11, 12) times

Loose Knots

Complex cables swoop in loose knots. This headband is sporty and playful, especially in a spotty colorway.

Sample in Koigu KPPM Fingering

Loose Knots

SIZES

Newborn (Baby, Toddler, Child, Adult SM, Adult LG) to fit heads 14 (16, 18, 20, 22, 24) in. / 35 (41, 46, 51, 56, 61) cm around

FINISHED MEASUREMENTS

Circumference: 12 (14, 16, 18, 20, 22) in. / 31 (36, 41, 46, 51, 56) cm

YARN

Koigu KPPPM; fingering weight; 100% merino wool; 175 yd. / 160 m per 1.7 oz. / 50 g skein
    1 skein #P454

YARN SUBSTITUTIONS

Try a smooth and bouncy fingering- or sport-weight yarn. Fuzzy or textured yarns may make the cables unclear; if you are going to spend time making cables, use a yarn that makes them pop!

NEEDLES AND GAUGE

Use needles for knitting flat, US 1 (2.25 mm) or whatever size makes a band 2.5 in. / 6 cm wide, measuring 1 in. / 2.5 cm below the needle once you have knit 4 in. / 10 cm.

PATTERN NOTES

• This headband is grafted together after knitting.

STITCHES AND SKILLS

Knit (k), purl (p), slip stitch (sl), cables (3/1 RPC, 3/1 LPC, 3/2 RPC, 3/2 LPC, 3/3 RC, 3/3 LC), provisional cast-on, and grafting.

PATTERN

Cast on 34 stitches using a provisional cast-on.

Work rows as below or following chart on page 50.
Row 1 (WS): Sl 3, [k4, p6, k4] twice, p3.
Row 2: Sl 3, [p4, 3/3 LC, p4] twice, k3.
Row 3: Sl 3, [k4, p6, k4] twice, p3.
Row 4: Sl 3, [p3, 3/1 RPC, 3/1 LPC, p3] twice, k3.
Row 5: Sl 3, [k3, (p3, k2) twice, k1] twice, p3.
Row 6: Sl 3, p3, k3, p2, 3/1 LPC, p4, 3/1 RPC, p2, k3, p3, k3.
Row 7: Sl 3, [(k3, p3) twice, k1] twice, k2, p3.
Row 8: Sl 3, p1, [p2, 3/1 LPC] twice, p2, [3/1 RPC, p2] twice, p1, k3.
Row 9: Sl 3, k1, [k3, p3] twice, k1, [k1, p3] twice, p2, k4, p3.
Row 10: Sl 3, p4, 3/2 LPC, p1, 3/1 LPC, 3/1 RPC, p1, 3/2 RPC, p4, k3.
Row 11: Sl 3, k6, [p3, k2, p3] twice, k6, p3.
Row 12: Sl 3, p6, 3/2 LPC, 3/3 RC, 3/2 RPC, p6, k3.
Row 13: Sl 3, k8, p12, k8, p3.
Row 14: Sl 3, p8, 3/3 LC twice, p8, k3.
Row 15: Sl 3, k8, p12, k8, p3.
Row 16: Sl 3, p7, 3/1 RPC, 3/3 RC, 3/1 LPC, p7, k3.
Row 17: Sl 3, k7, [p3, k1, p3] twice, k7, p3.
Row 18: Sl 3, p6, 3/1 RPC, p1, k6, p1, 3/1 LPC, p6, k3.
Row 19: Sl 3, k6, [p3, k2, p3] twice, k6, p3.
Row 20: Sl 3, p5, 3/1 RPC, p2, k6, p2, 3/1 LPC, p5, k3.
Row 21: Sl 3, k5, [p3, k3, p3] twice, k5, p3.
Row 22: Sl 3, p4, 3/1 RPC, p3, 3/3 RC, p3, 3/1 LPC, p4, k3.
Row 23: Sl 3, k4, [p3, k4, p3] twice, k4, p3.
Row 24: Sl 3, p3, 3/1 RPC, p2, 3/2 RPC, 3/2 LPC, p2, 3/1 LPC, p3, k3.
Row 25: Sl 3, k3, p4, [k2, p3, k2] twice, p4, k3, p3.
Row 26: Sl 3, p3, 3/1 LPC, 3/2 RPC, p4, 3/2 LPC, 3/1 RPC, p3, k3.
Row 27: Sl 3, [k4, p6, k4] twice, p3.
Repeat Rows 2–27 until band is 12 (14, 16, 18, 20, 22) in. / 31 (36, 41, 46, 51, 56) cm long. If one more repeat will make the band too long, stop knitting and let it be a little short instead.
Do not bind off. Pull out the provisional cast-on, place those stitches on a needle, and graft the ends of the band together.
Weave in yarn tails.

Wash the headband, and block it without pins.

Loose Knots

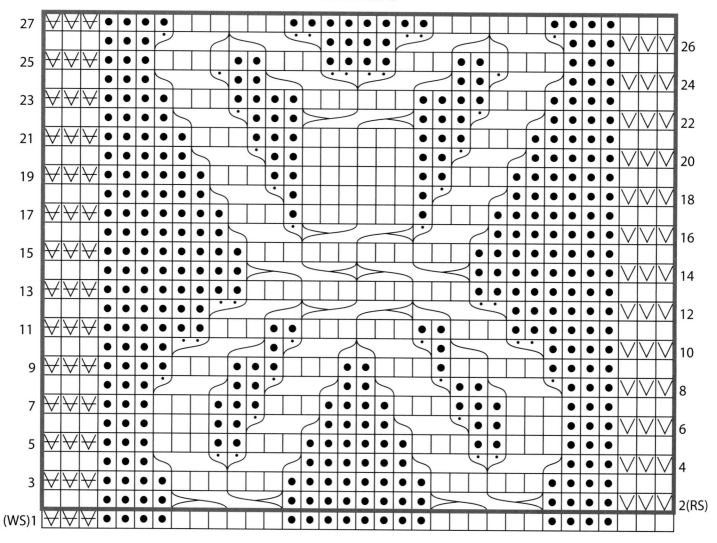

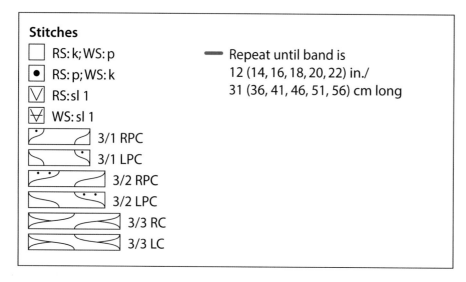

Stitches

☐ RS: k; WS: p

● RS: p; WS: k

V RS: sl 1

⋏ WS: sl 1

3/1 RPC

3/1 LPC

3/2 RPC

3/2 LPC

3/3 RC

3/3 LC

— Repeat until band is
12 (14, 16, 18, 20, 22) in./
31 (36, 41, 46, 51, 56) cm long

Lace
HEADBANDS

Leaf Garland

This simple stitch is lovely in all sorts of yarns, from a soft merino to a crisp linen chainette. Since the headband is tied, it is suitable for nonspringy yarns. When it stretches out, simply retie the knot to make it smaller.

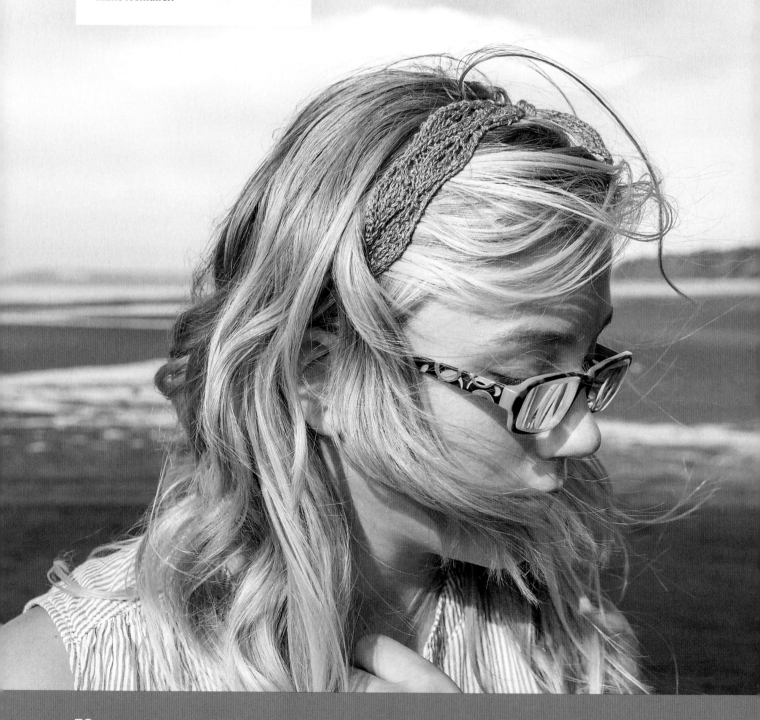

Top to bottom: Samples B (Shibui Linen Fingering) and A (Malabrigo Arroyo Sport)

Leaf Garland

SIZES
Newborn (Baby, Toddler, Child, Adult SM, Adult LG) to fit heads 14 (16, 18, 20, 22, 24) in. / 35 (41, 46, 51, 56, 61) cm around

FINISHED MEASUREMENTS
Width: 1½ in. / 4 cm in the middle, where the leaves are
Length: 16 (18, 20, 22, 24, 26) in. / 41 (46, 51, 56, 61, 66) cm

YARN
Sample A: Malabrigo Arroyo; sport weight; 100% super-wash merino; 335 yd. / 310 m per 3.5 oz. / 100 g skein
   1 skein #46 Prussia Blue
Sample B: Shibui Linen; fingering weight; 100% linen; 246 yd. / 225 m per 1.7 oz. / 50 g skein
   1 skein #2033 Cascade

YARN SUBSTITUTIONS
Try a lace-, fingering-, or sport-weight yarn that has good stitch definition.

NEEDLES AND GAUGE
Use needles for knitting flat, US 3 (3.25 mm) or whatever size makes a scarf 1½ in. / 4 cm wide, measuring 1 in. / 2.5 cm below the needle once you have knit about 6 in. / 15 cm.

PATTERN NOTES
- To wear the headband, wrap it around your head and tie a loose knot. Pull the scarf off gently (to avoid tying your hair into the knot), and then tighten and straighten out the knot.
- All of the decreases are k2tog or p2tog, making it easy if you don't like to ssk.
- Pay attention to the changing stitch count! If there is no new stitch count given, the count is the same as the row before.

STITCHES AND SKILLS
Knit (k), purl (p), slip stitch (sl), yarn over (yo), knit two together (k2tog), and purl two together (p2tog).

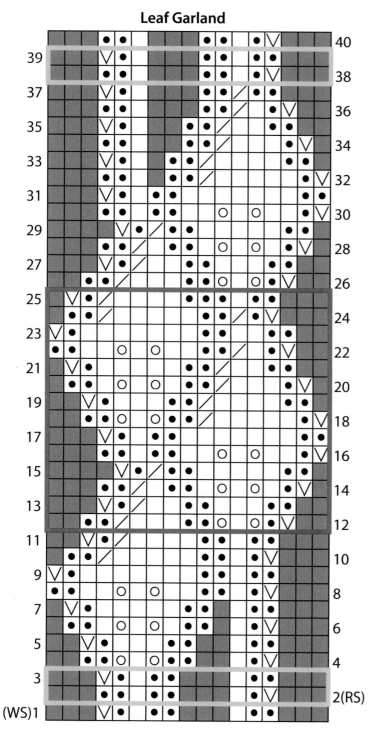

Leaf Garland

PATTERN

Cast on 8 stitches.

Row 1 (WS): Sl 1 wyif, [k1, p1, k1] twice, k1. (8 sts)
Row 2: Sl 1, [p1, k1, p1] twice, p1.
Row 3: Sl 1 wyif, [k1, p1, k1] twice, k1.
Repeat [Rows 2–3] 15 more times.
Row 4: Sl 1, p1, k1, p2, yo, k1, yo, p2. (10 sts)
Row 5: Sl 1 wyif, k1, p2, [p1, k2] twice.
Row 6: Sl 1, p1, k1, p2, k1, [yo, k1] twice, p2. (12 sts)
Row 7: Sl 1 wyif, k1, p4, [p1, k2] twice.
Row 8: Sl 1, p1, k1, p2, k2, [yo, k1] twice, k1, p2. (14 sts)
Row 9: Sl 1 wyif, k1, p6, [p1, k2] twice.
Row 10: Sl 1, p1, k1, p2, k5, k2tog, p2. (13 sts)
Row 11: Sl 1 wyif, k1, p2tog, p3, [p1, k2] twice. (12 sts)
Row 12: Sl 1, p1, yo, k1, yo, p2, k3, k2tog, p2. (13 sts)
Row 13: Sl 1 wyif, k1, p2tog, p2, k2, p3, k2. (12 sts)
Row 14: Sl 1, p1, k1, [yo, k1] twice, p2, k1, k2tog, p2. (13 sts)
Row 15: Sl 1 wyif, k1, p2tog, k2, p5, k2. (12 sts)
Row 16: Sl 1, p1, k2, [yo, k1] twice, [k1, p2] twice. (14 sts)
Row 17: Sl 1 wyif, k1, p1, k2, p7, k2.
Row 18: Sl 1, p1, k5, k2tog, p2, yo, k1, yo, p2. (15 sts)
Row 19: Sl 1 wyif, k1, p3, k2, p2tog, p4, k2. (14 sts)
Row 20: Sl 1, p1, k3, k2tog, p2, k1, [yo, k1] twice, p2. (15 sts)
Row 21: Sl 1 wyif, k1, p5, k2, p2tog, p2, k2. (14 sts)
Row 22: Sl 1, p1, k1, k2tog, p2, k2, [yo, k1] twice, k1, p2. (15 sts)
Row 23: Sl 1 wyif, k1, p5, [p2, k2] twice.
Row 24: Sl 1, p1, k2tog, p2, k5, k2tog, p2. (13 sts)
Row 25: Sl 1 wyif, k1, p2tog, p4, k3, p1, k2. (12 sts)
Repeat Rows 12–25 until headband is 11 (13, 15, 17, 19, 21)
    in. / 28 (33, 38, 43, 48, 53) cm long.

Stitches

▨	No stitch
☐	RS: k; WS: p
•	RS: p; WS: k
� V	RS: sl 1; WS: sl 1 wyif
○	yo
◪	RS: k2tog; WS: p2tog

— Work these rows 16 times
— Repeat until band is 11 (13, 15, 17, 19, 21)
    in./28 (33, 38, 43, 53) cm long

Row 26: Sl 1, p1, yo, k1, yo, p2, k3, k2tog, p2. (13 sts)

Row 27: Sl 1 wyif, k1, p2tog, p2, k2, p3, k2. (12 sts)

Row 28: Sl 1, p1, k1, [yo, k1] twice, p2, k1, k2tog, p2. (13 sts)

Row 29: Sl 1 wyif, k1, p2tog, k2, p5, k2. (12 sts)

Row 30: Sl 1, p1, k2, [yo, k1] twice, [k1, p2] twice. (14 sts)

Row 31: Sl 1 wyif, k1, p1, k2, p7, k2.

Row 32: Sl 1, p1, k5, k2tog, p2, k1, p2. (13 sts)

Row 33: Sl 1 wyif, k1, p1, k2, p2tog, p4, k2. (12 sts)

Row 34: Sl 1, p1, k3, k2tog, p2, k1, p2. (11 sts)

Row 35: Sl 1 wyif, k1, p1, k2, p2tog, p2, k2. (10 sts)

Row 36: Sl 1, p1, k1, k2tog, p2, k1, p2. (9 sts)

Row 37: Sl 1 wyif, k1, p1, k2, p2tog, k2. (8 sts)

Row 38: Sl 1, [p1, k1, p1] twice, p1.

Row 39: Sl 1 wyif, [k1, p1, k1] twice, k1.

Repeat [Rows 38–39] 15 more times.

Row 40: Sl 1, [p1, k1, p1] twice, p1.

Bind off.

Weave in yarn tails.

Wash the headband, and block it without pins.

Roman Lace Tie

This band is somewhere between a scarf and a "real" headband. The loose gauge means it knits up quickly, but be warned that it will take the first few rows for your fingers to get used to it. I have used two very different yarns: One is a firm hemp and cotton DK weight; the other is hand-dyed merino in fingering weight. Both are equally beautiful in this stitch, as many other yarns would be as well. Despite looking complex, the stitch is simple, using only knit and purl stitches with yarn overs and easy knit-two-together decreases.

Left to right: Samples B (RainCityKnits Variegated Fingering Sock 4-Ply) and A (Hemp for Knitting Hempton DK)

Roman Lace Tie

SIZES
To fit everyone (just tie it larger or smaller)

FINISHED MEASUREMENTS
Length: 28 in. / 71 cm
Width: 2 in. / 5 cm

YARN
Sample A: Hemp for Knitting Hempton; DK weight; 40% cotton, 30% hemp, 30% modal; 130 yd. / 120 m per 1.7 oz. / 50 g skein
   1 skein #071 Coral
Sample B: RainCityKnits Variegated Fingering Sock 4-Ply; fingering weight; 75% superwash merino wool, 25% nylon; 463 yd. / 423 m per 3.5 oz. / 100 g skein
   1 skein Graffiti

YARN SUBSTITUTIONS
Try any lace-weight yarn. The stretch in the stitch pattern and the fact that it is tied on will make even a nonstretchy yarn work out nicely. Use the same needle size and gauge as you would with the thicker yarns.

NEEDLES AND GAUGE
Use needles for knitting flat, US 7 (4.5 mm) or whatever size makes a scarf 2 in. / 5 cm wide, measuring along the cast-on edge once you have knit about 2 in. / 5 cm.

PATTERN NOTES
• This is a long rectangular scarf that is tied on.
• To wear the band, wrap it around your head and tie a loose knot. Pull the scarf off gently (to avoid tying your hair into the knot), and then tighten and straighten out the knot.
• This stitch pattern alternates between 18 and 10 stitches.

STITCHES AND SKILLS
Knit (k), purl (p), yarn over (yo), and knit two together (k2tog).

PATTERN

Cast on 10 stitches.

Row 1: [K1, yo] 8 times, k2. (18 sts)
Row 2: K1, p16, k1.
Row 3: K1, k2tog 8 times, k1. (10 sts)
Rows 4–5: K1, [yo, k2tog] 4 times, k1.
Rows 6–7: K10.
Row 8: [K1, yo] 8 times, k2. (18 sts)
Row 9: K1, p16, k1.
Row 10: K1, k2tog 8 times, k1. (10 sts)
Rows 11–12: K1, [yo, k2tog] 4 times, k1.
Rows 13–14: K10.
Row 15: [K1, yo] 8 times, k2. (18 sts)
Repeat Rows 2–15 until band is 28 in. / 71 cm long
Row 16: K1, p16, k1. (18 sts)
Bind off loosely.
Weave in yarn tails.

Wash headband and block it without pins.

Roman Lace Tie

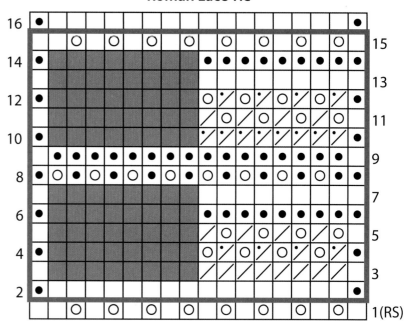

Stitches

▩ No stitch	— Repeat until scarf is 28 in./ 71 cm long
☐ RS: k; WS: p	
• RS: p; WS: k	
○ yo	
╱ RS: k2tog	
╱ WS: k2tog	

Bird's-Eye

This simple stitch lies perfectly flat without curling and stretches to fit around your head beautifully. Habu Textiles 4P is a smooth, nonstretchy yarn that seems limp and dull. Paired up with this stitch, it transforms into a slinky and stretchy net that snaps around your head in a satisfying manner.

Bird's-Eye

Sample in Habu
Textiles N-80 Wrapped
Merino 4P Fingering

SIZES
To fit everyone (just tie it larger or smaller)

FINISHED MEASUREMENTS
Length: 30 in. / 76 cm
Width: 4 in. / 10 cm

YARN
Habu Textiles N-80 Wrapped Merino 4P;
fingering weight; 99% merino, 1% fine silk;
187 yd. / 167 m per 1 oz. / 28 g skein
   1 skein #2 Mauve

YARN SUBSTITUTIONS
Try any lace- or fingering-weight yarn. The
stretch in the stitch pattern and the fact that
it is tied on will make even a nonstretchy yarn work out
nicely.

NEEDLES AND GAUGE
Use needles for knitting flat, US 7 (4.5 mm) or whatever
size makes a scarf 4 in. / 10 cm wide.

PATTERN NOTES
• This is a long rectangular scarf that is tied on.
• To wear the band, wrap it around your head and tie a
  loose knot. Pull the scarf off gently (to avoid tying your
  hair into the knot), and then tighten and straighten out
  the knot.
• The stitch pattern is simple, but the loose gauge makes
  it a little bit tricky, especially in the first few rows.

STITCHES AND SKILLS
Knit (k), purl (p), yarn over (yo), and
knit two together (k2tog).

PATTERN

Cast on 22 stitches.

Row 1 (WS): K1, k2tog, yo, [yo, k2tog twice, yo] 4 times, yo,
  k2tog, k1.
Row 2: [K3, p1] 5 times, k2.
Row 3: K3, [k2tog, yo twice, k2tog] 4 times, k3.
Row 4: K3, [k2, p1, k1] 4 times, k3.
Repeat Rows 1–4 until scarf is 30 in. / 76 cm long, or as long
  as desired.
Bind off.
Weave in yarn tails.

Wash headband, and block it without pins.

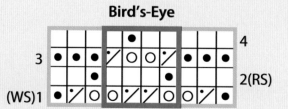

Bird's-Eye

Stitches
☐ RS: k
⊡ RS: p; WS: k
⊙ WS: yo
⧄ WS: k2tog

— Work 4 times across each row
— Repeat until band is
  30 in. / 76 cm long or as long as
  desired

Veined Leaf

Leaves pop out of a garter background in this simple but pretty headband.

Top to bottom: Samples A (Malabrigo Twist Aran)
and C (Patons Classic Wool DK Superwash); Sample B
(Knit Picks Wool of the Andes Superwash Bulky) shown on page 61

Veined Leaf

SIZES
Newborn (Baby, Toddler, Child, Adult SM, Adult LG) to fit
heads 14 (16, 18, 20, 22, 24) in. / 35 (41, 46, 51, 56, 61) cm
around

FINISHED MEASUREMENTS
Circumference: 11 (13, 15, 17, 19, 21) in. / 28 (33, 38, 43, 48,
53) cm

YARN
Sample A: Malabrigo Twist; Aran weight; 100% pure baby
merino wool; 150 yd. / 137 m per 3.5 oz. / 100 g skein
    1 skein #862 Piedras
Sample B: Knit Picks Wool of the Andes Superwash Bulky;
bulky weight; 100% superwash wool; 137 yd. / 125 m per
3.5 oz. / 100 g skein
    1 skein Celestial #26499
Sample C: Patons Classic Wool DK Superwash; DK weight;
100% superwash wool; 125 yd. / 114 m per 1.7 oz. / 50 g
skein
    1 skein #12200 Emerald

YARN SUBSTITUTIONS
Pick a springy yarn in worsted, Aran, or bulky weight.

NEEDLES AND GAUGE
Use needles for knitting flat, as follows:
    Worsted: US 8 (5 mm), or whatever size makes the band
2 in. / 5 cm wide
    Aran: US 10 (6.5 mm), or whatever size makes the band
2½ in. / 6 cm wide
Bulky: US 15 (10 mm), or whatever size makes the band
    3 in. / 7 cm wide

PATTERN NOTES
• This is a thin to thick, round headband.
• Cast on using a provisional cast-on that you can pull out
  later and graft the top to the bottom of the band.
• The thinnest area of the headband goes on the back of
  the head.
• The stitch count varies through the pattern.

STITCHES AND SKILLS
Knit (k); purl (p); yarn over (yo); knit two together (k2tog);
slip, slip, knit (ssk); slip two together, knit one, pass two
slipped stitches over (sl2tog-k1-p2sso); provisional cast-on;
and grafting.

PATTERN

Cast on 9 stitches using a provisional cast-on.

Work rows as below or follow chart on page 64.
Row 1: K3, [p1, k1] twice, k2. (9 sts)
Row 2: K4, p1, k4.
Repeat [Rows 1–2] 9 times.
Row 3: K3, p1, yo, k1, yo, p1, k3. (11 sts)
Row 4: K4, p3, k4.
Row 5: K3, p1, k1, [yo, k1] twice, p1, k3. (13 sts)
Row 6: K4, p5, k4.
Row 7: K3, p1, k2, [yo, k1] twice, k1, p1, k3. (15 sts)
Row 8: K4, p7, k4.
Row 9: K3, p1, ssk, k1, [yo, k1] twice, k2tog, p1, k3.
Row 10: K4, p7, k4.
Row 11: K3, p1, ssk, k3, k2tog, p1, k3. (13 sts)
Row 12: K4, p5, k4.
Row 13: K3, p1, ssk, k1, k2tog, p1, k3. (11 sts)
Row 14: K4, p3, k4.
Row 15: K3, p1, yo, sl2tog-k1-p2sso, yo, p1, k3.
Row 16: K4, p3, k4.

Row 17: K3, p1, k1, [yo, k1] twice, p1, k3. (13 sts)
Row 18: K4, p5, k4.
Row 19: K3, p1, k2, [yo, k1] twice, k1, p1, k3. (15 sts)
Row 20: K4, p7, k4.
Repeat Rows 9–20 until the headband is 10 (12, 14, 16, 18, 20) in. / 25 (30, 36, 41, 46, 51) cm long.
Row 21: K3, p1, ssk, k1, [yo, k1] twice, k2tog, p1, k3.
Row 22: K4, p7, k4.
Row 23: K3, p1, ssk, k3, k2tog, p1, k3. (13 sts)
Row 24: K4, p5, k4.
Row 25: K3, p1, ssk, k1, k2tog, p1, k3. (11 sts)
Row 26: K4, p3, k4.
Row 27: K3, p1, sl2tog-k1-p2sso, p1, k3. (9 sts)
Row 28: K4, p1, k4.
Row 29: K3, [p1, k1] twice, k2.
Do not bind off. Undo your provisional cast-on, and then graft the start and end of the headband together.
Weave in yarn tails.

Wash headband, and block it without pins.

Veined Leaf

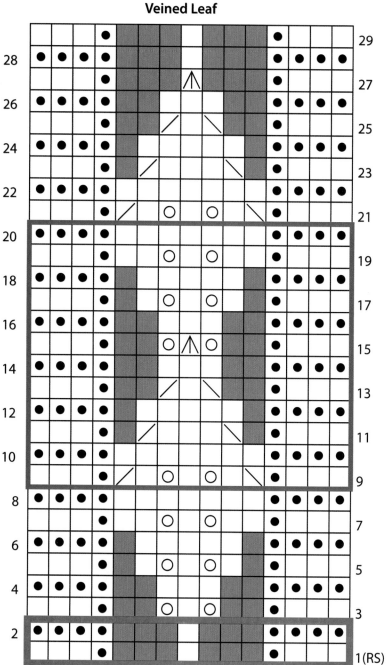

Stitches

⬛	No stitch	
⬜	RS: k; WS: p	
•	RS: p; WS: k	
O	yo	
╱	k2tog	
╲	ssk	
⋀	sl2tog-k1-p2sso	

— Work 10 times

— Repeat until band is
10 (12, 14, 15, 18, 20) in./
25 (30, 36, 41, 46, 51) cm long

Diagonal Mesh

This diagonally slanted mesh stitch is equally fun in a papery cotton and a summery self-striping Noro yarn. The stitch pattern slants and creates the pointy ends automatically. So easy!

Left to right: Samples B (Noro Taiyo Sock Fingering) and A (Habu Textiles A-174 Cotton Gima Lace)

Diagonal Mesh

SIZES
To fit everyone (just tie it larger or smaller)

FINISHED MEASUREMENTS
Length: 34 in. / 86 cm
Width: 5 in. / 13 cm

YARN
Sample A: Habu Textiles A-174 Cotton Gima; lace weight; 100% cotton; 265 yd. / 236 m per 1 oz. / 28 g cone
   1 cone #8(14)
Sample B: Noro Taiyo Sock; fingering weight; 50% cotton, 17% wool, 17% polyamide, 16% silk; 460 yd. / 420 m per 3.5 oz. / 100 g skein
   1 skein #S36

YARN SUBSTITUTIONS
Try any lace-weight yarn. The stretch in the stitch pattern and the fact that it is tied on will make even a nonstretchy yarn work out nicely.

NEEDLES AND GAUGE
Use needles for knitting flat, US 5 (3.75 mm) or whatever size makes a scarf 5 in. / 13 cm wide, measuring along the cast-on edge once you have knit about 2 in. / 5 cm.

PATTERN NOTES
- This is a long rectangular scarf that is tied on.
- To wear, wrap it around your head and tie a loose knot. Pull the scarf off gently (to avoid tying your hair into the knot), and then tighten and straighten out the knot.

STITCHES AND SKILLS
Knit (k), purl (p), yarn over (yo), knit two together (k2tog), and purl two together (p2tog).

PATTERN
Cast on 24 stitches.

Row 1 (WS): P24.
Rows 2–3: K24.
Row 4: K2, [k2tog, yo] 10 times, k2.
Row 5: P3, [yo, p2tog] 10 times, p1.
Row 6: P24.
Row 7: P2, [yo, p2tog] 10 times, p2.
Row 8: K1, [k2tog, yo] 10 times, k3.
Row 9: K24.
Repeat Rows 4–9 until band is 32 in. / 86 cm long, measuring along either edge.
Row 10: K24.
Row 11: P24.
Bind off.
Weave in yarn tails.

Wash headband, and block it without pins.

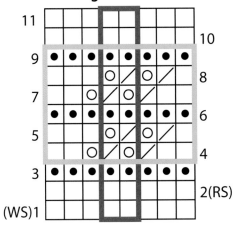

Diagonal Mesh

Stitches

☐ RS: k; WS: p	━ Work 9 times
● RS: p; WS: k	━ Repeat until sides are 32 in./86 cm long
⊙ yo	
⧄ RS: k2tog; WS: p2tog	

Waterfalls

The flow of this stitch is compelling, and it has just enough challenge to be fun, with pattern stitches on the right and wrong sides and a changing stitch count. Usually a cotton yarn is a bad choice for a fixed-length headband like this; cotton tends to stretch out over time and would often make a headband that is going to grow and slide off your head. Katia Cotton Stretch, though, has polyester spun into it to make it nice and springy and just perfect for a headband!

Left to right: Samples A (Katia Cotton Stretch DK) and B (Colour Adventures Dia Merino DK)

Waterfalls

SIZES
Newborn (Baby, Toddler, Child, Adult SM, Adult LG)

FINISHED MEASUREMENTS
Circumference: 12 (14, 16, 18, 20, 22) in. / 31 (36, 41, 46, 51, 56) cm

YARN
Sample A: Katia Cotton Stretch; DK weight; 87% cotton, 13% polyester; 186 yd. / 170 m per 1.75 oz. / 50 g skein
   1 skein #6 Beige
Sample B: Colour Adventures Dia Merino DK; DK weight; 100% superwash merino; 231 yd. / 211 m per 3.5 oz. / 100 g skein
   1 skein Serendipity

YARN SUBSTITUTIONS
Pick a springy yarn in sport or DK weight.

NEEDLES AND GAUGE
Use needles for knitting flat, US 2 (2.75 mm) or whatever size makes the band 1¾ in. / 4.5 cm wide once you have knit 2 in. / 5 cm.

PATTERN NOTES
• This headband is thin and round.
• This headband is knit flat, using a provisional cast-on. The cast-on is then pulled out, and the ends of the headband grafted together.

STITCHES AND SKILLS
Knit (k); purl (p); yarn over (yo); knit two together (k2tog); purl two together (p2tog); slip, slip, knit (ssk); slip, slip, purl (ssp); provisional cast-on; and grafting.

PATTERN

Cast on 12 stitches using a provisional cast-on.

Row 1 (WS): K2, [p3, k2] 2 times. (12 sts)
Row 2: P2, yo, k3, p2, k3, yo, p2. (14 sts)
Row 3: K2, [p4, k2] 2 times.
Row 4: P2, k1, yo, ssk, k1, p2, k1, k2tog, yo, k1, p2.
Row 5: K2, p2, p2tog, k2, ssp, p2, k2. (14 sts)
Row 6: P2, ssk, yo, k1, p2, k1, yo, k2tog, p2.
Repeat Rows 1–6 until the headband is 12 (14, 16, 18, 20, 22) in. / 31 (36, 41, 46, 51, 56) cm long.

Do not bind off. Undo the provisional cast-on, place those stitches on a knitting needle, and then graft the ends of the headband together.
Weave in yarn tails.

Wash the headband, and block it without pins.

Waterfalls

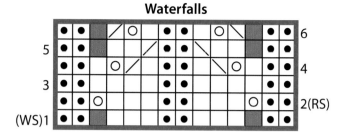

Stitches

▩ No stitch	— Repeat until band is 12 (14, 16, 18, 20, 22) in./ 31 (36, 41, 46, 51, 56) cm long
☐ RS: k; WS: p	
▣ RS: p; WS: k	
○ yo	
╱ RS: k2tog; WS: p2tog	
╲ RS: ssk; WS: ssp	

Palm Leaf

A simple mesh stitch has summery palm leaves in the middle. Thebe is a favorite yarn of mine, soft to the touch and with a fresh matte appearance. Stephanie from SpaceCadet created this color at my request last year, and I love it just as much now as I did when I opened the box and saw it for the first time.

Sample in SpaceCadet Thebe Lace

Palm Leaf

SIZES
To fit everyone (just tie it larger or smaller)

FINISHED MEASUREMENTS
Length: 35 in. / 89 cm
Width: 5 in. / 13 cm

YARN
SpaceCadet Thebe; lace weight; 65% cotton, 35% linen;
665 yd. / 608 m per 3.5 oz. / 100 g skein
    1 skein Sea Emerald

YARN SUBSTITUTIONS
Try any solid or heathered lace-weight yarn.

NEEDLES AND GAUGE
Use needles for knitting flat, US 5 (3.75 mm) or whatever
size makes a scarf 4½ in. / 11 cm wide, measuring 1 in.
/ 2.5 cm below the needle once you have knit about 5 in. /
13 cm.

PATTERN NOTES
• This headband is a long rectangular scarf that is tied on.
• To wear, wrap it around your head and tie a loose knot.
  Pull the scarf off gently (to avoid tying your hair in the
  knot), and then tighten and straighten out the knot.
• Once knit, block this scarf with pins so the stitch pattern
  shows better.

STITCHES AND SKILLS
Knit (k); purl (p); yarn over (yo); knit two together (k2tog);
purl two together (p2tog); knit through the back loop
(k-tbl); slip, slip, knit (ssk); and slip two together, knit one,
pass two slipped stitches over together (sl2tog-k1-p2sso).

PATTERN

Cast on 4 stitches.

Row 1: K4. (4 sts)

Row 2: P4.

Row 3: [K1, yo, k1] twice. (6 sts)

Row 4: P6.

Row 5: K2, [yo, k1] 3 times, k1. (9 sts)

Row 6: P9.

Row 7: K1, yo, k2, yo, sl2tog-k1-p2sso, yo, k2, yo, k1. (11 sts)

Row 8: P11.

Row 9: K1, [k1, yo] 3 times, sl2tog-k1-p2sso, [yo, k1] 3 times, k1. (15 sts)

Row 10: P15.

Row 11: K1, yo, k1, [yo, sl2tog-k1-p2sso, yo, k1] 3 times, yo, k1. (17 sts)

Row 12: P17.

Row 13: [K1, yo] twice, sl2tog-k1-p2sso, yo, k2, yo, k3, yo, k2, yo, sl2tog-k1-p2sso, [yo, k1] twice. (21 sts)

Row 14: P21.

Row 15: [K1, yo, k3, yo] twice, ssk, k1, k2tog, [yo, k3, yo, k1] twice. (27 sts)

Row 16: P27.

Row 17: Ssk, [yo, sl2tog-k1-p2sso] 3 times, [yo, k-tbl, yo, sl2tog-k1-p2sso] twice, yo, [sl2tog-k1-p2sso, yo] twice, k2tog. (21 sts)

Row 18: P21.

Row 19: Ssk, [yo, k1] twice, k1, k2tog, yo, k3, [yo, k1] twice, k2, yo, ssk, k1, [k1, yo] twice, k2tog. (25 sts)

Row 20: P25.

Row 21: K1, yo, [sl2tog-k1-p2sso, yo] twice, k2tog, k3, [yo, k1] twice, k2, ssk, yo, [sl2tog-k1-p2sso, yo] twice, k1. (23 sts)

Row 22: P23.

Row 23: K1, yo, k2, k2tog, yo, k2tog, k9, ssk, yo, ssk, k2, yo, k1. (23 sts)

Row 24: P23.

Row 25: Ssk, yo, sl2tog-k1-p2sso, yo, k-tbl, yo, ssk, k7, k2tog, yo, k-tbl, yo, sl2tog-k1-p2sso, yo, k2tog. (21 sts)

Row 26: P21.

Row 27: Ssk, [yo, k1] twice, k2, yo, ssk, k5, k2tog, yo, k2, [k1, yo] twice, k2tog. (23 sts)

Row 28: P23.

Row 29: K1, yo, [sl2tog-k1-p2sso, yo] twice, k-tbl, yo, ssk, k3, k2tog, yo, k-tbl, yo, [sl2tog-k1-p2sso, yo] twice, k1. (21 sts)

Row 30: P21.

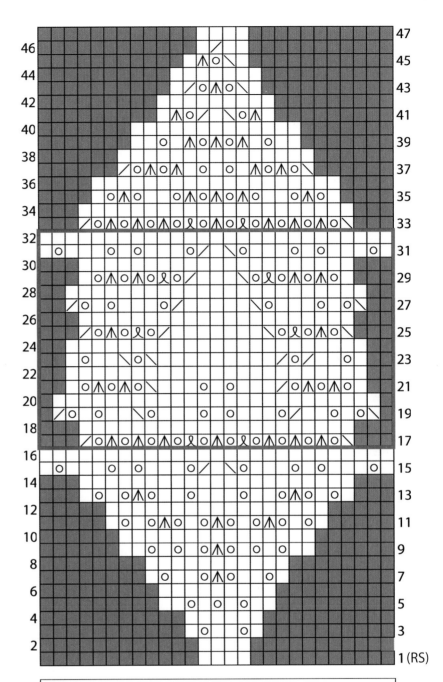

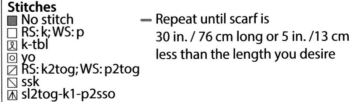

Stitches

- ⬛ No stitch
- ⬜ RS: k; WS: p
- ⊠ k-tbl
- ⊙ yo
- ⧄ RS: k2tog; WS: p2tog
- ⧅ ssk
- ⩘ sl2tog-k1-p2sso

— Repeat until scarf is 30 in. / 76 cm long or 5 in. / 13 cm less than the length you desire

Row 31: [K1, yo, k3, yo] twice, ssk, k1, k2tog, [yo, k3, yo, k1] twice. (27 sts)

Row 32: P27.

Repeat Rows 17–32 as many times as needed until scarf is approximately 30 in. / 76 cm long or 5 in. / 13 cm less than the length you desire.

Row 33: Ssk, [yo, sl2tog-k1-p2sso] 3 times, [yo, k-tbl, yo, sl2tog-k1-p2sso] twice, yo, [sl2tog-k1-p2sso, yo] twice, k2tog. (21 sts)

Row 34: P21.

Row 35: K1, yo, sl2tog-k1-p2sso, yo, k2, yo, [sl2tog-k1-p2sso, yo] 3 times, k2, yo, sl2tog-k1-p2sso, yo, k1. (19 sts)

Row 36: P19.

Row 37: Ssk, [yo, sl2tog-k1-p2sso] twice, k1, [yo, k1] twice, [sl2tog-k1-p2sso, yo] twice, k2tog. (15 sts)

Row 38: P15.

Row 39: K2, yo, k1, sl2tog-k1-p2sso, [yo, sl2tog-k1-p2sso] twice, k1, yo, k2. (13 sts)

Row 40: P13.

Row 41: K1, sl2tog-k1-p2sso, yo, ssk, k1, k2tog, yo, sl2tog-k1-p2sso, k1. (9 sts)

Row 42: P9.

Row 43: K1, ssk, yo, sl2tog-k1-p2sso, yo, k2tog, k1. (7 sts)

Row 44: P7.

Row 45: K1, ssk, yo, sl2tog-k1-p2sso, k1. (5 sts)

Row 46: P1, p2tog, p2. (4 sts)

Row 47: K4.

Bind off.

Weave in yarn tails.

Wash, and then block firmly. Pull the scarf in all directions to open up the stitch pattern, then stretch it out evenly, and pin it until dry.

Mini Chevron

Ready for a little challenge? This scarf uses a lovely and delicate stitch that has pattern stitches on the right and wrong sides. The stitch pattern is easy to follow, so it is a good choice for becoming comfortable with working a pattern on the wrong side. The pure silk yarn will feel slippery when you begin using it. You may want to use wood or bamboo needles. Once you make it through the first few rows, you will become accustomed to the silk. Give your fingers a little time to get used to it.

Sample in Euro Yarns Maharashtra Silk Lace

Mini Chevron

SIZES
To fit everyone (just tie it larger or smaller)

FINISHED MEASUREMENTS
Length: 38 in. / 97 cm
Width: 5 in. / 13 cm

YARN
Euro Yarns Maharashtra Silk; lace weight; 100% pure silk; 800 yd. / 731 m per 3.5 oz. / 100 g skein
  1 skein #5

YARN SUBSTITUTIONS
Try out your favorite multicolored lace-weight yarn. This stitch loves hand-dyed yarns!

NEEDLES AND GAUGE
Use needles for knitting flat, US 4 (3.5 mm) or whatever size makes a scarf 4 in. / 10 cm wide, measuring along the cast-on edge once you have knit about 4 in. / 10 cm.

PATTERN NOTES
• This band is a long rectangular scarf that is tied on.
• To wear, wrap it around your head and tie a loose knot. Pull the scarf off gently (to avoid tying your hair in the knot), and then tighten and straighten out the knot.
• Slippery yarns can be tricky. Work slowly for the first few rows until your fingers adapt.

STITCHES AND SKILLS
Knit (k); purl (p); yarn over (yo); knit two together (k2tog); purl two together (p2tog); slip, slip, knit (ssk); slip, slip, purl (ssp); slip two together, knit one, pass two slipped stitches over together (sl2-k1-p2sso); and slip two together, purl one, pass two slipped stitches over together (sl2-p1-p2sso).

PATTERN

Cast on 27 stitches.

Row 1: K1, ssk, k1, [yo, k1] twice, k2tog, k1, ssk, yo, k1, yo, sl2tog-k1-p2sso, yo, k1, yo, k2tog, k1, ssk, k1, [yo, k1] twice, k2tog, k1.

Row 2: P1, p2tog, p1, [yo, p1] twice, ssp, p2, p2tog, yo, p3, yo, ssp, p2, p2tog, p1, [yo, p1] twice, ssp, p1.

Row 3: K1, yo, ssk, k3, k2tog, yo, k1, yo, ssk twice, yo, k1, yo, k2tog twice, yo, k1, yo, ssk, k3, k2tog, yo, k1.

Row 4: P2, yo, p2tog, p1, ssp, yo, p3, yo, p2tog, p3, ssp, yo, p3, yo, p2tog, p1, ssp, yo, p2.

Row 5: K3, yo, sl2tog-k1-p2sso, yo, k5, yo, ssk, k1, k2tog, yo, k5, yo, sl2tog-k1-p2sso, yo, k3.

Row 6: P1, p2tog, p1, [yo, p1] twice, ssp, p1, p2tog, yo, p1, yo, sl2tog-p1-p2sso, yo, p1, yo, ssp, p1, p2tog, p1, [yo, p1] twice, ssp, p1.

Row 7: K1, ssk, k1, [yo, k1] twice, k2tog, k2, ssk, yo, k3, yo, k2tog, k2, ssk, k1, [yo, k1] twice, k2tog, k1.

Row 8: P1, yo, p2tog, p3, ssp, yo, p1, yo, p2tog twice, yo, p1, yo, ssp twice, yo, p1, yo, p2tog, p3, ssp, yo, p1.

Row 9: K2, yo, ssk, k1, k2tog, yo, k3, yo, ssk, k3, k2tog, yo, k3, yo, ssk, k1, k2tog, yo, k2.

Row 10: P3, yo, sl2tog-p1-p2sso, yo, p5, yo, p2tog, p1, ssp, yo, p5, yo, sl2tog-p1-p2sso, yo, p3.

Row 11: K1, ssk, k1, [yo, k1] twice, k2tog, k1, ssk, yo, k1, yo, sl2tog-k1-p2sso, yo, k1, yo, k2tog, k1, ssk, k1, [yo, k1] twice, k2tog, k1.

Repeat Rows 2–11 until band is 38 in. / 97 cm long.

Row 12: P1, p2tog, p1, [yo, p1] twice, ssp, p2, p2tog, yo, p3, yo, ssp, p2, p2tog, p1, [yo, p1] twice, ssp, p1.

Bind off.

Weave in yarn tails.

Wash headband and block gently without pins.

Mini Chevron

Stitches

- ☐ RS: k; WS: p
- ⟠ yo
- ╱ RS: k2tog; WS: p2tog
- ╲ RS: ssk; WS: ssp
- ⋀ RS: sl2tog-k1-p2sso; WS: sl2tog-p1-p2sso

— Repeat until scarf is 38 in. / 97 cm long

Colorwork
HEADBANDS

Diagonal Stripes

Increase on one side and decrease on the other, and your rows will slope over into diagonal stripes all on their own! Multicolored yarns will emphasize this effect, or use different colors of yarn for more precise stripes.

Left to right: Samples B (Yarn Ink Classic DK), C (Knit Picks Swish Worsted), and A (Malabrigo Merino Worsted)

Diagonal Stripes

SIZES
Newborn (Baby, Toddler, Child, Adult SM, Adult LG) to fit heads 14 (16, 18, 20, 22, 24) in. / 35 (41, 46, 51, 56, 61) cm around

FINISHED MEASUREMENTS
Circumference: 11 (13, 15, 17, 19, 21) in. / 28 (33, 38, 43, 48, 53) cm

YARN
Sample A: Malabrigo Merino Worsted; worsted weight; 100% merino wool; 210 yd. / 192 m per 3.5 oz. / 100 g skein
   1 skein #242 Amor Intenso
Sample B: Yarn Ink Classic DK; DK weight; 100% superwash merino wool; 256 yd. / 235 m per 4 oz. / 115 g skein
   1 skein Patina
Sample C: Knit Picks Swish Worsted; worsted weight; 100% superwash merino wool; 110 yd. / 100 m per 1.7 oz. / 50 g skein
   1 skein each Dove Heather, Conch, and Black

YARN SUBSTITUTIONS
Pick a springy yarn in DK, worsted, or Aran weight. This pattern works well with multicolored yarns or more than one yarn, but it will also work out nicely with a single solid or heathered yarn—it will still have diagonal stripes from the purled rows.

NEEDLES AND GAUGE
Use needles for knitting flat, US 6 (4 mm) or whatever size gives you a band 2½ in. / 7 cm wide once you have knit 6 in. / 15 cm. (Note that the cast-on edge and edge along the needle will be significantly longer.)

PATTERN NOTES
• Cast on using a provisional cast-on that you can pull out later and graft the top to the bottom of the band.

STITCHES AND SKILLS
Knit (k); purl (p); make one left (M1L); slip, slip, knit (ssk); provisional cast-on; and grafting.

PATTERN

Cast on 15 stitches using a provisional cast-on.

Row 1 (WS): P15.
Row 2: K1, M1L, k11, ssk, k1.
Row 3: K15.
Row 4: K1, M1L, k11, ssk, k1.
Row 5: P15.
Repeat Rows 2–5 until band is 11 (13, 15, 17, 19, 21) in. /
    28 (33, 38, 43, 48, 53) cm long.
Row 6: K1, M1L, k11, ssk, k1.
Row 7: K15.
Do not bind off. Undo your provisional cast-on, and then
    graft the start and end of the headband together.
Weave in yarn tails.

Wash the headband, and block it without pins.

Diagonal Stripes

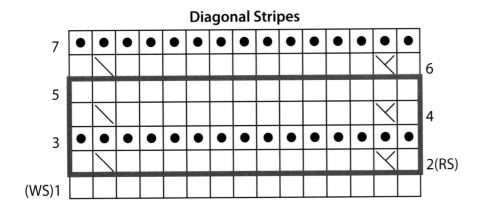

Stitches

☐ RS: k; WS: p   — Repeat until band is
● WS: k   11 (13, 15, 17, 19, 21) in. /
⊠ M1L   28 (33, 38, 43, 48, 53) cm long
◺ ssk

Chevron Stripes

Increases and decreases pull stitches over and, paired with a multicolor yarn, create chevron stripes!

Left to right: Samples B (Malabrigo Rastita DK) and A (Lion Brand Yarn Sock-Ease Fingering)

Chevron Stripes

SIZES

Newborn (Baby, Toddler, Child, Adult SM, Adult LG) to fit heads 14 (16, 18, 20, 22, 24) in. / 35 (41, 46, 51, 56, 61) cm around

FINISHED MEASUREMENTS

Circumference: 11 (13, 15, 17, 19, 21) in. / 28 (33, 38, 43, 48, 53) cm

YARN

Sample A: Lion Brand Yarn Sock-Ease; fingering weight; 75% wool, 25% nylon; 348 yd. / 400 m per 3.5 oz. / 100 g skein
  1 skein #201 Rock Candy
Sample B: Malabrigo Rastita; DK weight; 100% merino wool; 310 yd. / 285 m per 3.5 oz. / 100 g skein
  1 skein #146 Peacock

YARN SUBSTITUTIONS

Try any fingering, sport, or DK yarn. Self-striping or other nonsolid-colored yarns create the chevron effect, so pick your favorite stripy yarn!

NEEDLES AND GAUGE

Use needles for knitting flat, as follows:

Fingering: US 3 (3.25 mm) or whatever size makes a band 2.5 in. / 6 cm wide, measuring 1 in. / 2.5 cm below the needle once you have knit 6 in. / 15 cm.
DK: US 5 (3.75 mm) or whatever size makes a band 3 in. / 8 cm wide, measuring 1 in. / 2.5 cm below the needle once you have knit 6 in. / 15 cm.
Note: The band will seem much wider until it pulls inward, making the chevron, as you get the first inches knit.

PATTERN NOTES

• This headband is grafted together after knitting.
• Work the edge stitches loosely; they should be slightly looser than the middle stitches.
• The five-stitch decrease in the middle can be tricky, especially if you work tightly. If you struggle with it as written, instead try slipping four stitches purlwise to the right needle, knit the next stitch, and then pass the four stitches over the knit stitch one by one.

STITCHES AND SKILLS

Knit (k); purl (p); slip stitch (sl); make one (M1L, M1R); slip three together, knit two together, pass three slipped stitches over together (sl3tog-k2tog-p3sso); provisional cast-on; and grafting.

PATTERN

Cast on 25 stitches using a provisional cast-on.

Row 1 (WS): Sl 1, k1, p21, k1, p1.
Row 2: Sl 1, p1, [M1L, k3] twice, k2, sl3tog-k2tog-p3sso, k2, [k3, M1R] twice, p1, k1.
Row 3: Sl 1, k1, p21, k1, p1.
Row 4: Sl 1, p1, [k1, M1L, k2] twice, k2, sl3tog-k2tog-p3sso, k2, [k2, M1R, k1] twice, p1, k1.
Row 5: Sl 1, k1, p21, k1, p1.
Repeat Rows 2–5 until band is 11 (13, 15, 17, 19, 21) in. / 28 (33, 38, 43, 48, 53) cm long. Measure along one edge, and don't measure the point in the middle of the cast-on.
Row 6: Sl 1, p1, [M1L, k3] twice, k2, sl3tog-k2tog-p3sso, k2, [k3, M1R] twice, p1, k1.
Row 7: Sl 1, k1, p21, k1, p1.
Do not bind off. Pull out the provisional cast-on, place those stitches on a needle, and graft the ends of the band together.
Weave in yarn tails.

Wash the headband, and block it without pins.

Chevron Stripes

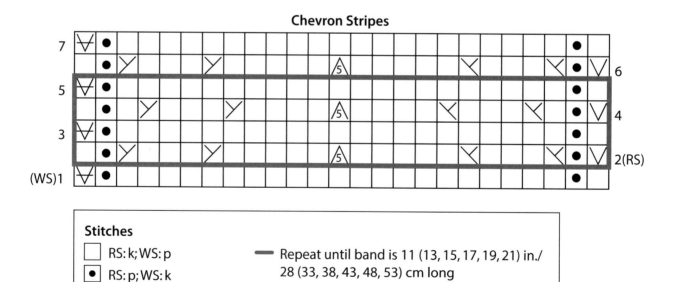

Stitches

- ☐ RS: k; WS: p
- ● RS: p; WS: k
- ⋁ RS: sl 1
- ⋏ WS: sl 1
- ⧄ M1R
- ⧅ M1L
- /5\ sl3tog-k2tog-p3sso

— Repeat until band is 11 (13, 15, 17, 19, 21) in./ 28 (33, 38, 43, 48, 53) cm long

Spotted You

If you have never done colorwork before, this is a great pattern to try first. It knits up superfast, and if you do something wrong it won't take too long to rip and restart. The most common mistake is pulling the yarn too tight between color changes—don't do this! You need a little bit of slack in the floats (the loops of unused yarn on the wrong side) for the headband to be able to stretch around your head.

Sample in Malabrigo Chunky Bulky

Spotted You

SIZES
Toddler (Child, Adult SM, Adult LG) to fit heads 18 (20, 22, 24) in. / 46 (51, 56, 61) cm around

FINISHED MEASUREMENTS
Circumference: 14 (16, 18, 20) in. / 36 (41, 46, 51, 56) cm
Width: 4 in. / 10 cm

YARN
Malabrigo Chunky; bulky weight; 100% merino; 100 yd. / 90 m per 3.5 oz. / 100 g skein
  1 skein each #093 Fucsia (A), #020 Cypress (B), and #130 Damask Rose (C)

YARN SUBSTITUTIONS
Try any bouncy chunky- or bulky-weight yarn that comes in three colors you like.

NEEDLES AND GAUGE
Use needles for knitting in the round, US 15 (10 mm) or whatever size gets you gauge. Because this headband is worked in the round, it is faster to make a swatch than to cast on and restart if it is not the right size. To swatch, cast on 12 stitches and work flat (back and forth) from the chart, making two repeats. Once your swatch is 3 in. / 8 cm long, measure about 1 in. / 2.5 cm below the needle, where it should be 4 in. / 10 cm wide.

PATTERN NOTES
• This headband is worked in the round.

STITCHES AND SKILLS
Knit (k), purl (p), stranded knitting, and working in the round.

Spotted You

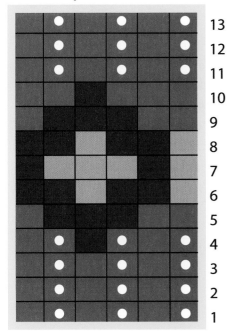

13
12
11
10
9
8
7
6
5
4
3
2
1

PATTERN

Cast on 42 (48, 54, 60) stitches in color A (Fucsia) and join in the round, being careful that there is not a twist in it.

Work from chart, repeating it across the round 7 (8, 9, 10) times.

Bind off loosely.

Weave in yarn tails.

Wash headband, and block it without pins.

■ Knit Color A   ⬤ Purl Color A   ▬ Work 7 (8, 9, 10) times around

■ Knit Color B

■ Knit Color C

Deep Sea

Far is a forgiving and stretchy chainette yarn. If you are not completely comfortable working with more than one color at once, Far is a good choice for its ability to even out messy stitches and uneven stranding. Besides being kind to beginners, Far is made of one of the softest merino wools available and feels wonderful against your forehead and ears.

Sample in Woolfolk Far Light Worsted

Deep Sea

SIZES
To fit child (adult) or heads 19–21 (21–24) in. / 48–53 (53–61) cm

FINISHED MEASUREMENTS
Width: 5 in. / 13 cm
Circumference: 18 (20.5) in. / 46 (52) cm

YARN
Woolfolk Far; light worsted weight; 100% Ovis 21 ultimate merino; 142 yd. / 130 m per 1.7 oz. / 50 g skein
   1 skein each in #10 (A, navy), #01 (B, white), and #09 (C, light blue)

YARN SUBSTITUTIONS
Try any springy, stretchy, worsted-weight yarn.

NEEDLES AND GAUGE
Use needles for knitting in the round, US 8 (5 mm) or whatever size gets you gauge. Because this headband is worked in the round, it is faster to make a swatch than to cast on and restart if it is not the right size. Cast on 26 stitches and work flat (back and forth) from the chart, making two repeats. Once your swatch is 3 in. / 8 cm long, measure about 1 in. / 2.5 cm above the cast-on edge, where it should be 5 in. / 13 cm wide.

PATTERN NOTES
• This headband is worked in the round.

STITCHES AND SKILLS
Knit (k), purl (p), stranded knitting, and working in the round.

PATTERN

Cast on 91 (104) stitches in color A (navy) and join in the round, being careful that there is not a twist in it.

Work Rows 1–28 from chart, repeating across the round 7 (8) times.

Bind off loosely.

Weave in yarn tails.

Wash the headband, and block it without pins.

Deep Sea

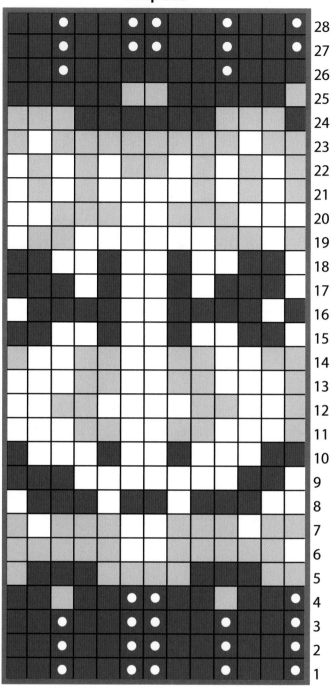

⬛ Knit Color A	▬ Work 7 (8) times around
⬜ Knit Color B	
⬜ Knit Color C	
⦿ Purl Color A	

Stripes

It might seem like more work to make a tube rather than a strip of fabric for this headband, but making a stockinette tube is a nice mindless activity (TV knitting, anyone?) and produces an irresistibly perfect result. I like to use a long circular needle and magic loop, but two circulars or double-pointed needles can also be used. Use the method you like for knitting small-circumference items.

Sample A is intentionally striped by changing colors. Sample B uses a multicolored yarn that makes stripes all by itself.

Left to right: Samples A (Knit Picks Stroll and Stroll Brights, Fingering) and B (Koigu KPPPM Fingering)

Stripes

SIZES
Newborn (Baby, Toddler, Child, Adult SM, Adult LG) to fit heads 14 (16, 18, 20, 22, 24) in. / 35 (41, 46, 51, 56, 61) cm around

FINISHED MEASUREMENTS
Circumference: 11 (13, 15, 17, 19, 21) in. / 28 (33, 38, 43, 48, 53) cm

YARN
Sample A: Knit Picks Stroll and Stroll Brights; fingering weight; 75% superwash merino wool, 25% nylon; 231 yd. / 211 m per 1.7 oz. / 50 g skein
   1 skein each Navy (MC), Blue Topaz (CC1), Highlighter Yellow (CC2), Pucker (CC3), Dove Heather (CC4), Hot Tamale (CC5), Electric Blue (CC6), and Vibrant Violet (CC7)
Sample B: Koigu KPPPM; fingering weight; 100% merino wool; 175 yd. / 160 m per 1.7 oz/ 50 g skein
   1 skein P718

YARN SUBSTITUTIONS
Pick a springy yarn in sport or DK weight.

NEEDLES AND GAUGE
Use needles for knitting in the round, US 3 (3.25 mm) or whatever size makes the band 1½ in. / 4 cm wide once you have knit 3 in. / 8 cm.

PATTERN NOTES
- This is a thin round headband—a stockinette tube. Cast on using a provisional cast-on that you can pull out later and graft the top to the bottom of the band.
- Hate grafting? Cast on with a regular cast-on, make the tube 5 in. / 13 cm longer, bind off, and tie a knot to wear it.
- If you are using just one color of yarn, simply ignore the color changes and knit away!

STITCHES AND SKILLS
Knit (k), knitting in the round, and changing colors.

PATTERN

Cast on 21 stitches using a provisional cast-on and join in the round, being careful not to twist the stitches.

Rounds 1–5: Knit in MC.

Round 6: Switch to CC1 and knit one round. Once the round is complete, cut CC1 and tie the tail from the start and end of this round (both CC1 tails) together, and trim the ends to ½–1 in. /1.5–2.5 cm long. Be careful as you tie that you don't pull the first and last stitches noticeably tighter than the other stitches. Don't cut the MC yarn at all.

Rounds 7–12: Knit in MC.

Round 13: Switch to CC2 for one round as in Round 6.

Continue in this way, working 6 rounds of MC and then one of the CCs, rotating through them in their number order. Keep going until the band is 11 (13, 15, 17, 19, 21) in. / 28 (33, 38, 43, 48, 53) cm long, ending with any CC round.

Do not bind off. Undo the provisional cast-on, place those stitches on a needle, and then graft the ends of the headband together using MC. All the yarn tails should be enclosed in the tube.

Wash the headband, and block it without pins.

Blowing Leaves

Pretty curved leaves almost seem to be blowing around this headband. This headband is doubly warm; after knitting it, you fold and stitch the cast-on edge to what would otherwise be the bind-off edge, hiding the back side of your colorwork. This makes the headband reversible, giving the option of a plain striped band or the leaf side.

Sample in Malabrigo Merino Worsted

Blowing Leaves

SIZES

To fit child (adult) or heads 19–21 (21–24) in. / 48–53 (53–61) cm. While you could work less repeats for a baby, the double layers of this headband might make it bulky on a tiny head, and that is why I have only two sizes.

FINISHED MEASUREMENTS

Circumference: 18 (21) in. / 46 (53) cm
Width: 3 in. / 8 cm

YARN

Malabrigo Merino Worsted; worsted weight; 100% merino wool; 210 yd. / 192 m per 1.7 oz. / 50 g skein
  1 skein each #135 Emerald (A) and #010 Fluo (B)

YARN SUBSTITUTIONS

Try any springy, stretchy, worsted-weight yarn that comes in two different colors. Especially if you are using tonal yarns, make sure one color is noticeably lighter/darker than the other, or the colorwork will not show the leaves distinctly.

NEEDLES AND GAUGE

Use needles for knitting in the round, US 8 (5 mm) or whatever size gets you gauge. Because this headband is worked in the round, it is faster to make a swatch than to cast on and restart if it is not the right size. Cast on 26 stitches and work flat (back and forth) from the chart, making two repeats. Once your swatch is 3 in. / 8 cm long, measure about 1 in. / 2.5 cm above the cast-on edge, where it should be 5 in. / 13 cm wide.

PATTERN NOTES

- This headband is worked in the round.
- After knitting, you fold the headband into a tube along the purl lines and graft it together with a long graft. Don't replace grafting with a three-needle bind-off or other "sewn" method of stitching for this headband—you need the stretch of grafting!

STITCHES AND SKILLS

Knit (k), purl (p), stranded knitting, working in the round, provisional cast-on, and grafting.

PATTERN

Using a provisional cast-on, cast on 91 (104) stitches in
color A (Emerald) and join in the round, being careful not
to twist the stitches.

Work Rounds 1–41 from the chart, repeating across the
round 7 (8) times.

Do not bind off. Undo your provisional cast-on and place
those stitches on a needle. Fold along the purl lines so
that the solid areas are covering the back side of the
colorwork and the edges are nearly touching. Graft the
start and end of the headband together with color B
(Fluo).

Weave in yarn tails.

Wash the headband, and block it without pins.

Blowing Leaves

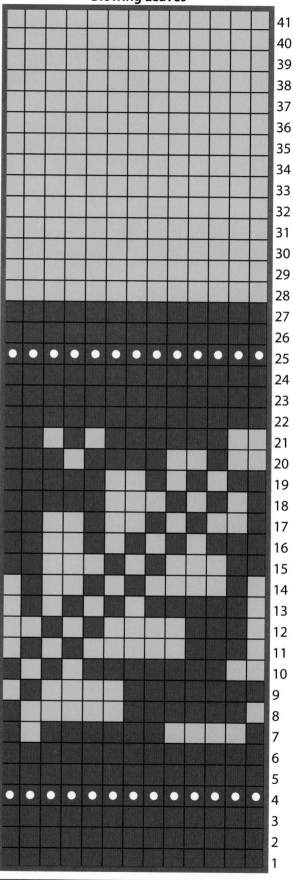

■ Knit Color A   ○ Purl Color A   ━━ Work 7 (8) times around
□ Knit Color B

Thistle

The wide repeat of the thistle motif makes this headband look complex—more complex than it really is. Unfortunately, this same feature means this headband doesn't work very well in more than one size, as each repeat of the chart adds or takes away 7 in. / 18 cm.

Sample in Drops Baby Merino

Thistle

SIZE
Adult, to fit heads 20–24 in. / 51–61 cm around

FINISHED MEASUREMENTS
Circumference: 21 in. / 53 cm
Width: 4 in. / 10 cm

YARN
Drops Baby Merino; fingering weight; 100% merino wool;
191 yd. / 175 m per 1.7 oz. / 50 g skein
   1 skein each #05 (A, light pink), #1 (B, white), #27
   (C, medium pink), and #30 (D, dark purple)

YARN SUBSTITUTIONS
Try a smooth fingering-weight yarn in solid or heathered
colors.

NEEDLES AND GAUGE
Use needles for knitting in the round, US 3 (3.25 mm) or
whatever size gets you gauge. Because this headband is
worked in the round, it is faster to make a swatch than
to cast on and restart if it is not the right size. Cast on 42
stitches and work flat (back and forth), making one repeat
from the chart. Once your swatch is 3 in. / 8 cm long, measure about 1 in. / 3 cm below the needle, where it should
be 7 in. / 18 cm wide.

PATTERN NOTES
• This headband is worked in the round.
• If you want to make the headband slightly smaller or
  larger, try using a smaller or larger needle size—this can
  shave off or add a couple inches.
• The colorwork has some long floats. Be sure to leave your
  yarn loose or the headband will pucker and, depending
  on how tight you pull the floats, you may not be able to
  pull it on.

STITCHES AND SKILLS
Knit (k), purl (p), stranded knitting, and working in the
round.

PATTERN

Cast on 126 stitches in color A (light pink) and join in the
round, being careful not to twist the stitches.

Work Rounds 1–31 from chart, repeating it across the round
3 times.

Bind off loosely.

Weave in yarn tails.

Wash the headband, and block it without pins.

Thistle

Knit Color A	Purl Color A
Knit Color B	Purl Color B
Knit Color C	Work 3 times around
Knit Color D	

Flame

I never understood why knitters obsessed over cashmere until I felt a shawl knit in a pure cashmere yarn, and I suddenly understood. You see, I had only ever felt cashmere in a blend. Pure cashmere is the loveliest thing you can imagine—you have to try it at least once! When you are using something so enjoyable as it slides through your fingers, you might as well take as long as you can, and so we have fine-weight colorwork here. The end result is worth every minute spent knitting.

Sample in Cashmered Yarn Fingering

Flame

SIZES
Newborn (Baby, Toddler, Child, Adult SM, Adult LG) to fit heads 14 (16, 18, 20, 22, 24) in. / 35 (41, 46, 51, 56, 61) cm around

FINISHED MEASUREMENTS
Circumference: 12½ (14, 15½, 18, 19½, 21) in. / 32 (36, 39, 46, 50, 53) cm
Width: 3 in. / 8 cm

YARN
Cashmered Yarn; fingering weight; 100% cashmere; 175 yd. / 160 m per .85 oz. / 25 g skein
  1 skein each Snowdrop (A, white), Natural (B, off-white), Caramel (C, beige), Chestnut (D, brown), and Strawberry (E, red)

YARN SUBSTITUTIONS
Try a smooth lace-weight yarn in solid or heathered colors.

NEEDLES AND GAUGE

Use needles for knitting in the round, US 1 (2.25 mm) or whatever size gets you gauge. Because this headband is worked in the round, it is faster to make a swatch than to cast on and restart if it is not the right size. Cast on 28 stitches and work flat (back and forth) from the chart, making two repeats. Once your swatch is 3 in. / 8 cm long, measure about 1 in. / 3 cm below the needle, where it should be just under 3 in. / 8 cm wide.

PATTERN NOTES

- This headband is worked in the round.
- The colorwork has some long floats. Be careful to leave your yarn loose or the headband will pucker and, depending on how tight you pull the floats, you may not be able to pull it on.

STITCHES AND SKILLS

Knit (k), purl (p), stranded knitting, and working in the round.

PATTERN

Cast on 126 (140, 154, 182, 196, 210) stitches in color B (Natural) and join in the round, being careful not to twist stitches.

Work Rounds 1–31 from chart, repeating it across the round 9 (10, 11, 13,14, 15) times.

Bind off loosely.

Weave in yarn tails.

Wash the headband, and block it without pins.

Flame

Legend:

☐ Knit Color A
☐ Knit Color B
▨ Knit Color C
■ Knit Color D
▩ Knit Color E
⦿ Purl Color B
— Repeat 9 (10, 11, 13, 14, 15) times

Stitches and Techniques

This section is intended to be a quick refresher on the techniques used in this book. If you aren't sure of a stitch or technique, I encourage you to look it up on YouTube; there are video tutorials on just about every stitch imaginable. Another favorite place to find in-depth descriptions and illustrations of knitting tricks and techniques is the TECHknitting blog: techknitting.blogspot.com.

STITCHES

Knit (k)

With yarn held in back of needles, insert right-hand needle through front of first loop on left needle, wrap yarn around the right needle, pull wrapped yarn through the stitch, pulling that stitch off the needle. The yarn that was wrapped around the right needle is now the new stitch.

Knit through the back loop (k-tbl)

Just like a regular knit stitch, but instead of putting the needle through the front "leg" of the stitch, put the needle through the back leg.

Knit two stitches together (k2tog)

Like a regular knit stitch, but put the needle through two stitches instead of one. This results in the left stitch overlapping the right, and on the next row, one stitch is decreased.

Knit three stitches together (k3tog)

Like a regular knit stitch, but put the needle through three stitches instead of one. This results in the left stitch overlapping the right and center, and on the next row, two stitches are decreased.

Knit, purl in one [(k,p) in 1]

Knit, leaving the stitch on the needle, and then purl into the same stitch.

Knit, purl, knit in one [(k, p, k) in 1]

Knit, leaving the stitch on the needle, then purl, and then knit into the same stitch.

Make one left (M1L)

From the front, lift the horizontal strand between stitches with the left needle. Knit through the back loop. You now have an extra stitch, the top of which leans toward the left.

Make one right (M1R)

From the back, lift the horizontal strand between stitches with the left needle. Knit through the front loop. You now have an extra stitch, the top of which leans toward the right.

No stitch

Shown on charts, a "no stitch" box indicates that there are less stitches on one row of a chart than on others. Simply move on to the next box on the chart that includes an instruction.

Purl (p)

With yarn held in front of needles, insert right-hand needle from back to front of first loop on left needle, wrap yarn around the right needle, pull wrapped yarn through the stitch, pulling that stitch off the needle. The yarn that was wrapped around the right needle is now the new stitch.

Purl two stitches together (p2tog)

Like a regular purl stitch, but put the needle through two stitches instead of one. This results in the left stitch overlapping the right, and on the next row, one stitch is decreased.

Purl, knit in one [(p, k) in 1]

Purl, leaving the stitch on the needle, and then knit into the same stitch.

Slip (sl)

With the working yarn in back, insert the right needle into the next stitch as if to purl, and transfer the stitch from the left needle to the right.

Slip one with yarn in front (sl 1 wyif)

With the working yarn in front, insert the right needle into the next stitch as if to purl, and transfer the stitch from the left needle to the right.

Slip, slip, knit (ssk)

Slip two stitches one at a time knitwise, insert the left-hand needle into the front loops of these stitches (left to right), then wrap the yarn as for a knit stitch, and knit the slipped stitches together. This will look just like a k2tog, but with the right stitch covering the left. One stitch decreased.

Slip, slip, purl (ssp)

Slip two stitches one at a time knitwise, then return slipped stitches to left needle, and purl the two stitches together through the back loop.

Slip two together, knit one, pass two slipped stitches over (sl2tog-k1-p2sso)

Slip two stitches together knitwise, knit one, and then pass slipped stitches over. The middle stitch overlaps the left and right stitch; on the next row you have one stitch where there used to be three (two stitches decreased).

Slip two together, purl one, pass two slipped stitches over (sl2tog-p1-p2sso)

Slip two stitches together knitwise, return slipped stitches to left needle, and then slip same two stitches together through back loop. Purl one, and then pass two slipped stitches over. Two stitches decreased.

Slip three together, knit two together, pass three slipped stitches over (sl3tog-k2tog-p3sso)

Slip three stitches together knitwise, knit two together, and then pass three slipped stitches over. Like the sl2tog-k1-p2sso, the center stitch overlaps, but this time it overlaps two stitches on each side, and on the next row you go from five stitches to one (four stitches decreased).

Yarn over (yo)

Wrap the working yarn over the right needle from front to back (counterclockwise). On the next row, knit into this loop as though it were a stitch.

CABLES

Cables all work the same way, using an extra needle to work the stitches out of order. I have photos on the next page of a 3/3 left and right cross; the only variation from them is the number of stitches held on the needle and worked before you go back to the cable needle.

1/1 LC (one over one left cross)
Slip 1 stitch to cable needle and hold in front; k1; k1 from cable needle.

1/1 LPC (one over one left purl cross)
Slip 1 stitch to cable needle and hold in front; p1; k1 from cable needle.

1/1 RC (one over one right cross)
Slip 1 stitch to cable needle and hold in back; k1; k1 from cable needle.

1/1 RPC (one over one right purl cross)
Slip 1 stitch to cable needle and hold in back; k1; p1 from cable needle.

1/2 LC (one over two left cross)
Slip 1 stitch to cable needle and hold in front; k2; k1 from cable needle.

1/2 RC (one over two right cross)
Slip 2 stitches to cable needle and hold in back; k1; k2 from cable needle.

2/2 LC (two over two left cross)
Slip 2 stitches to cable needle and hold in front; k2; k2 from cable needle.

2/2 RC (two over two right cross)
Slip 2 stitches to cable needle and hold in back; k2; k2 from cable needle.

3/1 LPC (three over one left purl cross)
Slip 3 stitches to cable needle and hold in front; p1; k3 from cable needle.

3/1 RPC (three over one right purl cross)
Slip 1 stitch to cable needle and hold in back; k3; p1 from cable needle.

3/2 LC (three over two left cross)
Slip 3 stitches to cable needle and hold in front; k2; k3 from cable needle.

3/2 LPC (three over two left purl cross)
Slip 3 stitches to cable needle and hold in front; p2; k3 from cable needle.

3/2 RC (three over two right cross)
Slip 2 stitches to cable needle and hold in back; k3; k2 from cable needle.

3/2 RPC (three over two right purl cross)
Slip 2 stitches to cable needle and hold in back; k3; p2 from cable needle.

3/3 LC (three over three left cross)
Slip 3 stitches to cable needle and hold in front; k3; k3 from cable needle.

3/3 RC (three over three right cross)
Slip 3 stitches to cable needle and hold in back; k3; k3 from cable needle.

TECHNIQUES

Blocking

Fill a sink/bowl with tepid water and a small squirt of hand washing detergent.

Soak the headband for about 10 minutes. Squish it gently in the water, and check to see if the water is strongly colored. If the wash water has noticeable color in it, pull the headband out, drain, replace the wash water, and soak another 10 minutes. Still bleeding? Keep soaking and squishing in new bowls of water (after the first two, don't bother with more soap, but keep the temperature of the water the same) until the water is clear or only lightly colored. Once you have (or if you started with) clear or light water, squeeze out as much water as you can with your hands, but don't wring it. (For faster drying, lay the headband flat on a towel, roll it up, and jump on the roll to pull even more water out.) Gently pull the headband width and lengthwise a couple times, alternating. Lay flat on a dry towel, and spread it flat with your fingers. Straighten the sides so they are smooth. I try to err on the side of making the headband too wide rather than too long—as soon as you wear it, it'll stretch out to the length you need—but do spread it in both directions, as far as it will stay on its own. (If you want it crisper or want to really make your scalloped edges pop, lay your towel on a foam board or even on the couch and use pins to spread the fabric as far as it goes.)

Your headband will take 12–48 hours to dry, depending on how wet it was to start and the humidity and airflow in your house. If you want to speed it up, set up a house fan to blow gently over the headband (I usually find that a fan cuts drying time in half or to a quarter), move the headband to a new towel or different area of the same towel that is dry every 4 or so hours (cuts out a couple hours of drying time) and flip it so both sides get turns facing up, and/or place it in direct sunlight (not recommended for regular use as sunlight will gradually weaken the fibers, but when you just need your headband dry soon, sometimes you don't care and on a hot sunny day, this can dramatically reduce drying time).

Once fully dry, give the headband a gentle shake to fluff it up, and you are good to go!

Grafting

This is stockinette grafting, also known as the Kitchener stitch. It looks like stockinette, or knitting, on the right side of the piece. If you don't like to graft, feel free to substitute three-needle bind-off, or start your headband with a regular cast-on and then finish by binding off and sewing the ends together.

With needles parallel and the wrong sides of the knitting together, hold the needle with the live stitches at the top and the needle with the stitches from the provisional cast-on at the bottom. You will have one less stitch on the picked up edge.

Using a tapestry needle, thread your yarn through the first stitch on the bottom needle, knitwise, left to right, leaving the stitch on the (knitting) needle.

1. On the top needle, thread your needle purlwise through the first stitch and pull the stitch off the needle. Then pull your needle knitwise through the next stitch. Pull the yarn until it is slightly tighter between the knitting needles than your tension in the headband.

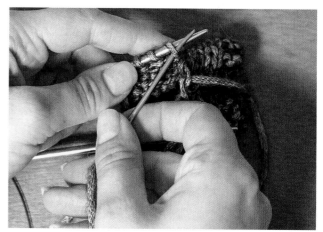

2. On the bottom needle, thread your needle knitwise through the first stitch and pull the stitch off the needle. Then pull your needle purlwise through the next stitch. Pull the yarn until it is slightly tighter between the knitting needles than your tension in the headband.

Repeat steps 1–2 until all the stitches are off the knitting needles.

Provisional cast-on

There are a few ways to work a provisional cast-on; use the one you like best. My favorite method for headbands is to cast on (using any cast-on you prefer) using scrap yarn, preferably a smooth cotton, and then knit one row on top of it with my working yarn. When it's time to undo the cast-on, I pick up each stitch in the working yarn and then cut the cast-on edge off. This can be time-consuming when used on a large project, but for a small one like a headband, it goes by quickly, and there's no risk of dropping stitches.

Yarn Sources

The yarns in this book are sourced from everywhere: Some can only be found online, others in local yarn shops, and still others in big-box craft shops. If you can't find a certain yarn, try asking the owner of your local yarn shop. If the yarn is not in stock, the owner might be willing to order some in just for you.

Berroco • berroco.com

Yarn used in book: Ultra Alpaca Chunky

Cashmered • cashmered.net

Pure cashmere, in one weight. You just can't go wrong with cashmere! I love Cashmered for its modern, fun colors, which can be hard to find in pure cashmere.

Colour Adventures • anadiomenadesigns.blogspot.ca

One of my local dyers with some seriously gorgeous colorways!

Yarn used in book: Dia Merino DK

Diamond • diamondyarn.ca

Yarn used in book: Pima Lino Lace

Drops • garnstudio.com

Lots of basic yarns in really pretty colors. I want all the colors!

Yarn used in book: Baby Merino

Euro Yarns • knittingfever.com/brand/euro-yarns

Yarn used in book: Maharashtra Silk

Filatura di Crosa • filaturadicrosa.com

Yarn used in book: Chiné

Habu Textiles • habutextiles.com

Sourced in Japan, Habu has the most unique yarns. Who else makes yarn that looks exactly like paper?

Yarn used in book: Wool Crepe N-90, N-80 Wrapped Merino 4P, A-174 Cotton Gima

Hemp for Knitting • lanaknits.com

Yarn used in book: Hempton

HiKoo • skacelknitting.com

Yarn used in book: Kenzie

Hoooked • hoooked.co.uk

One of the brands that makes T-shirt yarn, and in a huge variety of colors and prints!

Yarn used in book: Zpagetti

Istex • istex.is/english

Icelandic wool—low twist, long fiber staple, in modern neutrals and brights.

Yarn used in book: Álafosslopi

Katia • katia.com

Yarn used in book: Cotton Stretch

Knit Picks • knitpicks.com

For affordable natural fiber yarns, Knit Picks is my favorite. I think they have the nicest yarns (and colors!) in their price range.

Yarn used in book: Reverie, The Big Cozy, Capra, Stroll and Stroll Brights, Wool of the Andes, and Swish

Koigu · koigu.com

The very first "yarn-store yarn" I ever bought was a pair of green skeins of Koigu, and I still love Koigu as much as I did back then. The way the yarn is stretchy and springy, the playful colors . . . it is hard to walk by a Koigu wall and not buy a handful!

Yarn used in book: KPPPM

KPC Yarn · kpcyarn.com

This is a new company to me. It is located in Hong Kong, and the yarns are the type used for luxury machine-knit sweaters. They are high-twist, multi-ply, with luxurious drape. Of all the yarns I have bought, my KPC box had the most thoughtful packaging, from the brochure with care instructions to the ribbon keeping the balls together, and the price is very affordable.

Yarn used in book: Cashmere 4 Ply

Lang Yarns · langyarns.com

Yarn used in book: Asia

Lion Brand · lionbrand.com

I tend to shop online for yarn, but when I stop by the local big-box craft stores, Lion Brand yarn is what I find filling my bag.

Yarn used in book: Amazing, Alpine Wool, Sock-Ease

Louet · louet.com

Yarn used in book: Euroflax

Malabrigo · malabrigoyarn.com

Have I ever been to a local yarn store that didn't carry Malabrigo? I don't think so, and it is for a good reason. Malabrigo is equally famous for the softness of their merino wool and the beauty of their kettle dyes: a win-win for the knitter!

Yarn used in book: Rasta, Merino Worsted, Arroyo, Twist, Rastita, Chunky

Noro · noroyarns.com

Noro has their own secret processes for creating long-color-change yarns, and they have some of the most unique fiber blends as well. They have something of a cult following, and I don't think anyone else has mastered this type of yarn quite like they have.

Yarn used in book: Cyochin, Taiyo /Sock

Patons · www.yarnspirations.com/patons

Yarn used: Kroy Socks, Classic Wool DK Superwash

RainCityKnits · raincityknits.com

Gorgeous colors. Few things make me feel as happy as seeing a bundle of RainCity's bright, happy yarn!

Yarn used in book: Superwash Merino Worsted, High Twist DK, Variegated Fingering Sock 4-Ply

Schachenmayr · us.schachenmayr.com

Yarn used in book: Original Boston

Shibui · shibuiknits.com

Some of the most unique luxury yarns are found with Shibui. Whenever they come out with a new yarn line I can't help but buy a skein to swatch with just to see how it works.

Yarn used in book: MAAI, Linen

Shulana · loveknitting.com/us/schulana-knitting-yarn

Yarn used in book: Mersilca

SpaceCadet · spacecadetyarn.com

I have enjoyed working with Stephanie at SpaceCadet more than once, and her yarn bases really are unique and interesting to work with, not to mention the colors!

Yarn used in book: Thebe

Sweet Fiber · sweetfiberyarns.com

Yarn used in book: Canadian

Woolfolk · woolfolkyarn.com

Ultrafine merino wool. Need I say more? The velvety softness of cashmere and the spring of merino—I love it.

Yarn used in book: Tynd, Far

Yarn Ink · yarnink.com

I am picky about hand-dyed yarns—I don't like many of them. Yarn Ink makes gorgeous colorways. I went through their display, meaning to buy one—and ended up with three because I just couldn't choose between them.

Yarn used in book: Superwash DK

Visual Index

Garter 2

1x1 Ribbed 5

I-Cord 8

Shaped Garter Bulky 11

Seeds 15

I-Cord Garter 18

Waves 22

Simple Cable 28

Braid 31

X & O Cables 34

Round About 37

Bamboo Cables 40

Labyrinth 43

Loose Knots 47

Leaf Garland 52

Roman Lace Tie 56

Bird's-Eye 59

Veined Leaf 61

Diagonal Mesh 65

Waterfalls 68

Palm Leaf 71

Mini Chevron 75